A SOCIAL HISTORY OF THE SCOTCH-IRISH

OTHER BOOKS BY CARLTON JACKSON

Presidential Vetoes

Zane Grey, 2nd edition, 1989

J. I. Rodale: Apostle of Nonconformity

The Great Lili

The Dreadful Month

Hounds of the Road

Who Will Take Our Children? The Story of the British Evacuation 1935–1945

Hattie: The Life of Hattie McDaniel

AS COAUTHOR

Foundations of Freedom

Challenge and Change

Two Centuries of Progress, 3rd edition, 1990

AS EDITOR

Zane Grey, George Washington, Frontiersman

A Social History of THE SCOTCH-IRISH

Carlton Jackson

MADISON BOOKS
LANHAM • NEW YORK • LONDON

First paperback printing 1999

Published by Madison Books
4720 Boston Way
Lanham, Maryland 20706

12 Hid's Copse Road
Cumnor Hill, Oxford OX2 9JJ, England

Distributed by National Book Network

The Library of Congress catalogued the cloth edition of this work as follows:
Jackson, Carlton.
A social history of the Scotch-Irish / Carlton Jackson.
p. cm.
Includes bibliographical references and index.
1. Scots-Irish—United States—History. I. Title.
E184.S4J33 1992
973'.049163—dc20 92-26455 CIP

ISBN 0-8191-8071-8 (cloth : alk. paper)
ISBN 1-56833-142-8 (pbk. : alk. paper)

The paper used in this publication meets the minimum requirements of American National Standard for Information Sciences—Permanence of Paper for Printed Library Materials, ANSI/NISO Z39.48–1992.
Manufactured in the United States of America.

This book is dedicated to
my sisters, Lois Shipp, Pearl McLeroy,
Vernell Paine, Jean Mathews, and Vonda Bearden,
and my brothers,
Robert and James Jackson,
and to Elvie's memory—
good Irish all.

Contents

Foreword

Second to the English, the Scotch-Irish were the most numerous English-speaking settlers in British North America from 1720 to 1783. In the colonial period they ultimately ranged all the way from New Hampshire to Georgia, and in postrevolutionary times they expanded even further. Today some twenty-two million Americans claim Scotch-Irish descent.

The Scotch-Irish originated primarily in the Scottish Lowlands and first began going to north Ireland in the early seventeenth century at the behest of King James I, himself a Scotsman. He wanted the Lowlanders to be "God's bulldogs," he said, "to bite the wild Irish" into submission to English authority. His Ulster Plantation began a process of bitterness between the Protestant North and the Catholic South in Ireland that continues to this day.

To get away from the religious, economic, and military troubles affecting Ireland, many thousands of Ulstermen opted to leave the Old Country and come to British North America. Beyond appointing a commission in the 1720s to study why there was so much emigration from northern Ireland, the English Parliament made little effort to stem the flow of departures. In fact, while France was England's enemy in the New World, the Scotch-Irish were encouraged to go, because they were such good fighters and frontiersmen.

How many Scotch-Irish ultimately made their way to British

North America? In his Pulitzer Prize-winning *Voyagers To The West,* Bernard Bailyn writes: "There is no realistic figure for Scotch-Irish immigration before 1760. James G. Leyburn, *The Scotch-Irish: A Social History* . . . accepts the traditional estimate of 200,000 between 1717 and 1775. . . . R. J. Dickson, *Ulster Emigration to Colonial America, 1718–1775,* provides estimates of ship departures from Ireland for scattered groups of years that total about 65,000. Other statements go as high as 300,000. The traditional figure used here seems a reasonable minimum."[1] After the Revolution, as I shall show, there were additional Scotch-Irish immigrations so that by the end of the War of 1812 a fair estimate of *total* Scotch-Irish who came to North America would be approximately 350,000.

Winthrop D. Jordon, in *White Over Black: American Attitudes Toward The Negro, 1550–1812,* reported that "the best available estimate is that in 1790 between 61 and 66 percent of white Americans were of English origin and that between 80 and 84 percent were of English speaking origin."[2] The census of 1790 did not break down Americans into ethnic groups other than black and white. Louis B. Wright, in *The Cultural Life of the American Colonies, 1607–1763* said, "The most careful study of the distribution of population on the basis of national origins was that made in 1927 by a group of scholars under the auspices of the American Council of Learned Societies (ACLS), using the statistics of the first federal census of 1790. This study, using linguistic techniques in the analysis of family names, revealed that of the total white population of 3,172,444 in the United States, 60.9 percent were English, 14.3 percent were Scotch and Scotch-Irish from Ulster . . ."[3]

Apparently, the ACLS study of 1927 took similar-sounding names and grouped them together as Scotch and Scotch-Irish. If, however, we take Leyburn's "reasonable minimum" of 200,000 and split the difference with Bailyn's "other estimates" of 300,000, we can reasonably guess that some 250,000 Scotch-Irish were in America at the close of the Revolution in the early 1780s. Many reputable historians, Maury Klein and Maldwyn Jones among them, have stated that between the end of the Revolution and 1813 some additional 100,000 Scotch-

Irish came to the United States, an average of about 3,300 per year. If we take that yearly average for the seven years between 1783, when the Revolution ended and 1790, when the first federal census was conducted, we can estimate that some additional 23,100 Scotch-Irish were in the country, which would bring the total to 273,000 people. If 14.3 percent of white Americans in 1790 were of Scotch and Scotch-Irish origins, these figures reveal that 8.6 percent of them were Scotch-Irish (273,000 is roughly 8.6 percent of 3,172,444) and 5.7 percent were Scotch. This percentage puts the Scotch-Irish slightly ahead of the Germans who, in the 1927 ACLS study, were said to amount to about 8.3 percent of the American population.

David Doyle, however, in his respected work *Ireland, Irishmen, and Revolutionary America,* puts the percentage of Scotch-Irish in 1790 even higher. "Studies of nomenclature revealed by the first federal census (1790) suggest that 9% of the American people were ethnic Scots-Irish, a figure later adjusted downwards [by whom the author does not say], but which was somewhat an underestimate. . . . If corrections are made, it is probable that the Scots-Irish in 1790 were as many as 11% of New Yorkers, 21% of Pennsylvanians, 11% of Marylanders, 14% of Virginians, 13% of North Carolinians, 24% of South Carolinians, and 27% of Georgians."[4] These were the states with the highest numbers of Scotch-Irish and, if one accepts Doyle's figures, the percentage here was approximately 17 percent of the total population of these states. When adding all the other states where Scotch-Irish settled, either abundantly or sparsely, his overall average falls to about 10 percent. Obviously, then, to compute the number of Scotch-Irish descendants in 1790 is less than an exact procedure. Possibly, the best that can be done is to say that in 1790 between 8.6 and 10 percent of Americans were of Scotch-Irish origin.

Bernard Bailyn, in *The Peopling of British North America,* speaks at length about the dynamics of immigration, pointing out that the Scotch-Irish, like most other immigrants of the time, were "people in motion" even before they came to the shores of America.

> The first movements to America from Scotland and Ireland, whenever they occurred, were not different from those from England, from the German states, from Switzerland, or from the Low Countries. In the early phases of the migrations the existing *patterns* of mobility in these homelands were unaffected by the American magnet. . . . The North American colonies were simply another destination available to people in motion. But in time the dynamics of the situation changed. Everywhere, though in different phasings, the pull of the American colonies grew to the point where it shaped the patterns of European domestic mobility.[5]

Thus, one may say that the Scotch-Irish were used to moving about while they were still in the Old World. When economic, political, and religious conditions became intolerable in the Old Country, the mobility tendency of the Scotch-Irish practically assured their immigrations in large numbers to the North American continent.

To be sure, Scotch-Irish immigration to North America and their experiences on the continent itself have to be studied and considered in the context of other nationalities who immigrated. The Scotch-Irish, with some 8.6 percent of the total population by 1790, were definitely a minority, but they were a minority whose influence was sometimes stronger than their numbers, particularly in reference to the Revolution and the making of the Constitution. Well before the Revolution erupted in 1775, there had been skirmishes between predominantly Scotch-Irish settlers in the southern backwoods and the British authorities. Certainly the Scotch-Irish were not principally responsible for creating the Constitution in 1787, but the fact remains that the checks and balances system was quite acceptable to most of the Scotch-Irish, who were fairly well committed to Presbyterian hierarchical systems of appeal. The Scotch-Irish, as I shall try to demonstrate, *played a role* in creating the Revolution and the Constitution.

Nor were all Scotch-Irish "good." Many of them had a ruthless nature, especially against the American Indian, whom they regarded as an impediment to "civilized" progress. Many were slaveholders but not to the extent of their more coastal English neighbors. As Winthrop D. Jordon observed, "In the eighteenth century Negroes were heavily concentrated on the seaboard of the southern half of the English territory along the Atlantic edge of the North American continent. . . . The movement of slaves onto new lands [however] lagged markedly behind the pace of western settlement."[6] It appears, then, that wherever the Scotch-Irish owned slaves, they were not primarily the plantation owners but worked alongside their slaves out in the fields and elsewhere. It is also true that the Scotch-Irish contributed many undesirable elements to American society. In the nineteenth century the Ku Klux Klan was founded by men of Scotch-Irish descent. Then, too, such famous renegades and outlaws as Simon Girty, the James Brothers, the Youngers, and the Daltons, were all of Scotch-Irish stock; their individual histories, however, go beyond the scope of this work. In truth, the Scotch-Irish were similar to other immigrant groups; they were not "good" or "bad" but a combination of both, perhaps with a slightly greater proclivity for frontier life than others.

In this study I am primarily concerned with those people who came from Ulster—the ones whose ancestors originated mostly in the Scottish Lowlands. I am aware that some authors do not distinguish between "Irish" and "Scotch-Irish." Whether one should or should not make such distinction is not the main question here—though I do discuss it to some extent in the text. What I want to impress upon the reader is that I am talking in this book about north Ireland, and I am talking about south Ireland only to the extent that it has any bearing on Ulster. Also, the dates covered by this study are approximately from the time the Ulster Plantation started, around 1610, to the ten- to- fifteen year period following the War of 1812. Thus, the subject I am pursuing comes to an end around 1830. I do not discuss, except in passing, the tremendous influx of persons from the whole of Ireland, caused by the potato famines later in the century.

The Scotch-Irish came first to Massachusetts but, finding themselves treated inhospitably by the Puritans, they went on to Pennsylvania; and the southern part of Lancaster County then became the usual destination of those who followed. From there, the Scotch-Irish spread out through Maryland, Virginia, the two Carolinas, and Georgia. Everywhere they went, they were greeted with a mixture of foreboding and respect. They became known as claims-jumpers in the places they previously visited. Although they were also highly religious people, they could shoot straight if they thought someone meant them harm.

When people have written about the Scotch-Irish, they sometimes claim that the Revolution extinguished them as an ethnic group. They kept coming in large numbers, however, well after the Revolution. From the end of the Revolution into the 1840s, a fair estimate of Scotch-Irish (not including the Irish) immigrants who came to the United States would be 150,000. Thus, the assimilation process came later than the Revolution; it was more the War of 1812 than the Revolution that slowed down their arrivals—at least temporarily—and caused the assimilation process. Even after the War of 1812, however, the Scotch-Irish kept coming; some authorities have said that twice as many came between the Revolution and 1850 as during the colonial period (not a particularly startling revelation in view of the failures of Ireland's potato crops).[7] Terry Coleman reported in *Going to America* that the ten-year period from 1846 to 1855 "saw by far the greatest emigration from the United Kingdom to America known till then."[8]

When I started research on *A Social History of the Scotch-Irish,* I wrote to several small-town newspapers around the country, especially in Pennsylvania, asking their readers to supply me with some Scotch-Irish anecdotes. The response was quite positive, and I want to mention one small dispute that arose. Is the proper term "Scotch-Irish" or is it "Scots-Irish"? One correspondent mentioned that her late mother's pet peeve was the use of the phrase "Scotch-Irish" and added that if her mother were still around, she would give me "what-for." "Scotch," I was told, is either an adjective or an alcoholic drink. Perhaps one could argue, however, that only the first generation of Lowland Scots who settled in Ulster could be called "Scots-Irish" because in that case both "Scots" and "Irish" would be nouns. After the first generation, one might say that those people were Irish of primarily Scottish descent; therefore, the adjective "Scotch" would be appropriate. Probably the argument will continue as long as people remember those Scottish-derived Ulstermen who decided to come to the New World.

In this book I have tried to describe simply and accurately the experiences of the Ulstermen in Ireland who became the Scotch-Irish in America. Chapter One recounts the setting in Scotland and the reasons why James I wanted to establish the Ulster Plantation. Chapter Two deals with the growing troubles between Ulstermen and the English Parliament which led to the decisions of thousands to come to British North America. Chapter Three describes crossing the Atlantic by the Scotch-Irish, some of the dangers they faced, and the tragedies that sometimes befell them. Chapter Four shows how the Scotch-Irish first came to Massachusetts and, after being rebuffed by the Puritans, began their travels again—this time into Pennsylvania. In due course, New Castle, Delaware, and nearby Philadelphia became the major ports of entry for the Scotch-Irish as well as large numbers of other immigrant groups. The fifth chapter is an explication of Scotch-Irish movement out of Lancaster County, Pennsylvania, into the western and southern regions. Chapter Six deals with Scotch-Irish ways of life, and their religious, social, and folkloristic beliefs. The Revolution and the making of the Constitution comprise the subject matter of Chapter Seven. Chapter Eight traces Scotch-Irish history from the end of the Revolution to about 1830 and tries to show some contemporary efforts to commemorate the deeds of the Scotch-Irish in America.

A substantial portion of the research for this book came from original materials. I was fortunate to spend quite some time in Belfast, which, in spite of its troubles, has become one of my favorite cities. One day I was talking with a young Ulster lad in Belfast, and he said he thought it was time for the descendants of all those Ulstermen who *did* go to North America to change places with the descendants of all those Ulstermen who *did not* go to America. "Turnabout is fair play," he said.

I was able to use the resources at the Public Record Office of North Ireland (PRONI) while in Belfast, and I wish to thank Brian Follis and the staff there for their courtesies and assistance. There were many personal letters, diaries, and notebooks of people of the seventeenth and eighteenth centuries who expressed their views on immigration to the New World. I used the *Belfast Newsletter* at the Linen Hall Library, where Mary Duffey and Mary Hughes were very helpful and courteous.

In Kew, London, I used the Colonial Office records which dealt with American opinion of the French at the beginning of the Revolution. I thank my many friends at the Kew Public Record Office for their continued support of my work; the PRO at Kew is, in my opinion, the best research place in the world.

In the United States I traveled from South Carolina to Pennsylvania in the spring of 1988 gathering Scotch-Irish materials. I thank my friends Ross and Ruth Webb of Rock Hill, South Carolina, for their hospitality while I worked at Winthrop College. At the Presbyterian Historical Foundation in Montreat, North Carolina, I found much material and much hospitality from the staff; at the University of North Carolina, John White was most helpful as was Linda McCurdy at Duke University. I found a great deal of material at the Augusta County, Virginia, Historical Society, as well as at the Pennsylvania Historical Society, the Presbyterian Historical Society, Temple University and the Balch Institute. I thank all the people who had a hand in helping me to collect material. I certainly do extend my appreciation to the Southern Regional Education Board in Atlanta for its grant in aid that made the U.S. trips possible.

While it is true that I leaned heavily on original materials for this book, I tried not to bypass the latest scholarship in secondary sources. Though there are many studies of the Scotch-Irish today in the form of seminars and learned papers, the last academic book to come out on them as they existed in Scotland, Ireland, and America, was James G. Leyburn's *The Scotch-Irish: A Social History,* published in 1962 (reprinted in paperback in 1989). Numerous books dealing with national and local history published since 1962 do make references to the Scotch-Irish, as do, generally speaking, all the standard U.S. history textbooks. The materials were so vast—at least in the form of mentioning the Scotch-Irish for a paragraph or two and then moving on to other subjects—that I had carefully to choose what I would use from the secondary materials available. If I have not included a source or theme that some specialists might deem crucial to my study, it is probably not because I overlooked it but rather because I had to be selective.

At Western Kentucky University, I was aided by grants from the research committee, and I thank each member of that committee. My friends and colleagues, Professors Helen Crocker, Lowell Harrison, Drew Harrington, and Richard Stone read the manuscript either entirely or in part and offered helpful suggestions. My student assistant, David McCord, performed many useful tasks for which I am grateful. In further research on this subject students Matthew Jackson and Benjamin Hutchins at the University of Helsinki were helpful. Susan Gore and her staff at the Western Kentucky University Library interloan department gave me their full cooperation and support.

Finally, I take pleasure, once again, in thanking members of my family for their continued support: Pat, Beverly and Steve; Dan and Grace; Hilary; Matthew; and Colleen, Megan, Kate, Travis, Patrick, and Austin.

Carlton Jackson
History Department
Western Kentucky University

CHAPTER ONE

The Beginnings: From Scotland to Ireland

Scotland's geography has largely determined its character and history. It is divided geographically, linquistically, and culturally into two parts, the Highlands, and the Lowlands.

The Highlands is the larger of the two parts, encompassing most of the territory north of the River Clyde where rugged mountains caused isolated clans to originate and flourish. The areas of Inverness, Aberdeen, Kincardine, Angus, Argyll, and Perth make up a substantial portion of the Highlands. The geographical separation of one Highland clan from another contributed to the sense of independence Scotsmen developed. The Highlanders were hostile to Scottish governmental agents of law and order trying to control them.[1]

It was a hard matter to eke out food crops in the rocky, unfriendly soil of northern Scotland. The countryside's ruggedness rubbed off on the Highlanders and made them stoic, deterministic people. Perhaps that condition encouraged the Highlanders during the sixteenth and early seventeenth centuries to raid the Lowlanders, and sometimes even go across the border into England.[2]

As a rule, the Lowlanders despised the Highlanders, faulting them for their lawless ways and war-like manners. The Highlanders remained preeminently Celtic, while there were numerous influxes of Danes, Saxons, and Flemish—besides the Angles—in the Lowlands.[3] Much Celtic influence was felt in both parts of Scotland and, according to some scholars, accounted for the chief differences between Scotland and England. "It is a basic distinction between Scot and Englishman that the Scot in greater or less degree is a Celt."[4] In turn, this distinction marked the difference between a Highlander and a Lowlander; the Highlander spoke Celtic while the Lowlander generally spoke English.[5]

Geographical factors dictated against any strong nationalism in the Highlands. The clans, separated by hills and mountains, tended to be loyal unto themselves, a loyalty that produced individualism and a fear and distrust of outsiders. The clan leaders were feudalistic lords with the trappings of an entire feudal structure at their bid and command. Many Highlanders, seeking to avoid the harsh existence that their poor farms offered, became militaristic, frequently serving as mercenaries in the army of some powerful country like France.

The Scottish Lowlands comprise the southern and eastern parts of the country. The area is funnel shaped, with the narrow end jutting out into the North Channel of the Irish Sea, in places not more than twenty miles from the mainland of north Ireland. The counties embraced by the Lowlands include Stirling, Renfrew, Roxburgh, Lanark, Edinburgh, Linlithgow, Haddington, Berwick, Selkirk, Peebles, Ayr,[6] Wigton, Kircudbright, and Dumfries.

The Lowlanders resembled the north English in many significant ways—language and attitudes toward legal authority, for example—particularly those from the border counties of Northumberland, Cumberland, Westmoreland, Durham, Lancashire, and Yorkshire. In the immigration to north Ireland in the early seventeenth century, a large contingent of Englishmen also went to Ulster. Frequently, no distinction was made in these journeys between the Lowlander and the "Up Country" Englishman.

Agriculture in Scotland

The best agricultural lands in Scotland were in the Plains of Lothian in the Lowlands. These lands were mostly barren of trees, hedges, and other foliage, though landowners frequently planted clumps of ash, elm, and sycamores around their houses for shelter.[7] The crops were mostly grains—barley, some wheat, and above all else, oats. Oaten cakes have long been a staple in Scotland, for both humans and animals.

The cattle and sheep industry grew minimally in the western Lowlands, notably around Ayrshire.[8] (Cattle were generally smaller in Scotland than in England, for a lack of hay).[9] Some coal (called blackstone) and peat constituted most of Scotland's mineral resources. These agricultural and industrial resources were augmented by fishing and gaming.

For the most part, seventeenth century life in Scotland, both Highland and Lowland, was bleak, desolate, and isolated. Under the feudal structure, arable land was divided into "infield" and "outfield," the former the nearest to the home, the latter the farthest away. The same crops were planted on these fields year after year with little effort to improve the soil by rotation farming, and the chief fertilizers were cow and sheep manures. The poor soil, in addition to the frequent wet seasons resulted in impaired, late harvests, and caused the Lowlanders as much as the Highlanders to grub out a miserable living. An additional land problem was the uncertainty of leases. With few exceptions, leases were too short and doubtful of renewal to encourage tenants to improve their holdings.[10] The result was that farm land, none too fertile to begin with, became increasingly worse.

The Lowlander became more a migrant than the Highlander. He frequently traveled, hoping to find a better piece of land upon which to support his family. He often participated in foreign wars to supplement his and his family's lot.

Thus, long before the Lowland Scots made their way to Ulster and then to North America, they were a restless lot. They already had the immigrant frame of mind which, through a combination of poor economic conditions, religious persecutions, and military adventurism, led them away from their native country. Historian Wallace Notestein argued that the Scots were "roving stock" in part because they were fishermen and not afraid to venture from their own shores. More importantly though, the Scot, who had so few resources in his country, "had imagination enough to guess that he might better his chances by seeking out richer countries."[11]

Lowlanders and Highlanders: Some Differences

A major difference between the Highlander and the Lowlander was their attitude toward organized government. The feudal structure in north Scotland dictated against the growth of nationalism. There was not in the Lowlands, however, the uniformity that the clan system imposed on the Highlands.[12] The influx of diverse peoples (Flemings, Norse, Saxons, Angles), prevented any one group from gaining dominance. Their attitudes toward government were not as stringent as in the Highlands. The proximity of the Lowlands to England accounted to some extent for the Lowlanders' feelings toward government; they acquired many of the north English characteristics, which ultimately caused the Lowlanders to have a greater affinity with the English than with the Highland Scots.

Even so, the Lowlanders developed a strong sense of individualism, inculcating feelings of self-reliance. The hard farming life they led, the disastrous crop years they frequently experienced, and the terrible shortages they often suffered inured them to providing for themselves rather than looking to government or other sources when they had a problem.

Nonetheless, the Lowlander was more amenable to accepting laws and regulations than his Highland counterpart. One wonders what would have happened if the latter day Tudors and early Stuarts had tried to colonize the Highlanders into Ulster; undoubtedly, the chances for success would have been diminished.

Outsider Views of Scotland

Both Highlanders and Lowlanders were held in low esteem by continental visitors as well as by the English. By and large, the Scotsman was regarded as miserly.[13] Surely the hand to mouth existence of most Scots caused them to value material possessions; at the least, little if anything would be thrown away. Things were too hard to come by for Scots to be careless or wasteful with them, and perhaps their attitude was based not so much on miserliness as on conservancy. Outsiders, though, continued to see them as stingy and mean, missing any semblance of a cheerful countenance. One traveler to Scotland in the eighteenth century gave this uncomplimentary picture: "The air [in Scotland] might be wholesome but for the stinking people that inhabit it; the ground might be fruitful had they wit to manure it."[14] Another traveler, an Englishman returning home, exclaimed about Scotland: "I passed to English ground, and hope I may never go to such a country again. I thank God I never saw such another."[15]

According to some travelers, the Scots—both Highland and Lowland—ate raw fish, and as for their butter and cheese, one wrote, "I will not meddle withal at this time, nor no man else who loves his life."[16] The Scots apparently believed it was unlucky to wash their churns (superstition was especially rife among the Highlanders); they frequently put live frogs into the churn to make the butter, and the consistency of their butter was often determined by the number of hairs (both human and animal) in it.[17] Strange ways, these, remarked one traveler after another. But what could one expect, asked a visitor, from a people whose finest garden flower was a thistle?[18] (Other plants treasured by Scots besides the thistle included basil, hyssop, camomile, horehound, cat-mint, elocampine, and turnips, called "neeps".)[19]

Getting up time for Scotsmen in the seventeenth century was between 5 and 6 A.M., with breakfast at 8. Watered gruel ("skink") was common, accompanied by oaten cakes. The noonday meal, called dinner, was light, featuring the ever-present oaten cake and ale. In the early eighteenth century, tea was introduced to the consternation of many "purist" Scotsmen; it was a "foreign" drink, a "new-fangled, effeminate folly" that caught on in England more quickly than in Scotland.[20] The evening meal, called supper, was the big dining event of the day. In the summer or fall, there were usually great quantities of fresh mutton, (called "callops,") and fish. In the winter and spring Scotsmen relied on salted meat—usually mutton—supplemented occasionally with beef.

No matter the main course, it was always washed down with prodigious quantities of ale—accompanied sometimes in the wealthier homes by fine claret. Even after dinner, the host and guests were apt to keep drinking. Ian Finlay noted that the Lowlander usually got "unpleasantly drunk" at his meals because "he never had the chance to relax and discover the true meaning of leisure."[21]

Meal decorum apparently got so out of hand that schoolmaster Adam Petrie had to lay down rules of etiquette. These "rules of good deportment for the use of youth" required one to drink from one's own glass, and not to gnaw bones too cleanly, fill the mouth too full, suck meat from a spoon, throw anything on the floor, or wipe one's nose with a table napkin.[22] Even when the Scotch-Irish reached North America, their eating habits were frequently described by "genteel" folk as "disgusting."

With the exception of a few wealthy people, most Scotsmen lived in houses that were little better than hovels. These vermin-infested buildings hosted humans and animals alike—frequently for mutual warmth. It was a never-ending battle; the beleaguered farmers kept stuffing the cracks and holes in their little huts with bracken to keep out strong wintry blasts. They could not have fires to speak of, since the land was virtually timberless; the most used substance for heating was peat, and it was not available in great abundance.[23] The best a Scotsman could do in the dead of winter was snuggle up to his favorite cow and pray for an early spring.

The bad winters, coupled with a lack of heat and a sparsity of clothing, made the Scot vulnerable to a number of maladies. Each year, illnesses like smallpox, rheumatism, malaria, and the black death, took a dreadful toll.[24] All this misery helped to put Scotsmen into a fatalistic frame of mind, and to believe that God visited these things upon them for some sin, known or unknown. In time, however, it helped to cause thousands of Lowlanders to think about leaving the country.

Religion in Scotland

Religion played an important role in the lives of most Scotsmen. Christianity in Scotland dated from the sixth and seventh centuries, with the conversion works of Saints Columba and Cuthbert.[25]

Presbyterianism triumphed in 1567, with the work of Protestant reformer John Knox, who preached original sin, predestination, and a stern retribution for wrongdoing.[26] Ministers of the Kirk (the Scottish word for church, to distinguish from the Church of England and the Scottish Episcopal Church) instilled feelings of puritanical severity into their followers.[27] Thus, the Protestant Reformation of the sixteenth century was harsher and more intense in Scotland than in other parts of Europe, perhaps because the rigors of Calvinism had discouraged in Scotland the artistic and scientific advances brought on by the Renaissance in many other European countries.

The Scottish Reformation produced an unyielding hatred of Roman Catholicism, a hatred that influenced much subsequent Scotch-Irish history. Scots believed that the best road to heaven was any that did not go through Rome, and that to disbelieve the Pope and his Catholic hierarchy was the most efficient way to serve God. The Scotch Presbyterians did not, however, embody doctrines of separation of church and state. They believed that government officials should also be ministers or elders of the church. To vote or hold office, one had to be the owner of property.

The Scottish Presbyterians believed in the infallibility of the scriptures, and this doctrine, more than any other, was responsible for the close attention Scotsmen ultimately paid to education. They believed it was incumbent on the good Christian to become literate so he could read and learn from inerrant scripture. This feeling of personal responsibility for education was another indication of Scottish individualism. As a result of their religious faith, the Scots started—at least in theory—a tradition of education before any other country of Europe.[28] John Knox insisted upon a school in every parish; (although this did not always occur.) The result was an intellectual pattern "supported by the warm co-operation of parents, teachers, and the authorities. . . . A greater proportion of Scots, probably, than of any other people can boast of a higher education in the purely academic sense."[29] Scotland's educational system grew to such lengths that "as early as 1576 it was proposed that Gaelic-speaking Scots should be imported to preach to the Irish."[30]

On the eve of the Ulster migration Scotsmen could be individualists, religious fanatics with an anti-Papal bent, and determinists. They were also superstitious, and possessed a love of learning for religious purposes. The physical milieux in which they practiced these ways of life were far from desirable: mountainous terrains, which intensified a sense of isolation and rugged soils, and only begrudgingly yielded food enough to support a Scotsman and his family. Under such conditions, whenever a Lowlander had a chance to travel or immigrate, he usually grabbed the opportunity.

The Ulster migration of the early seventeenth century provided two important things to the Lowland Scot. It gave him a way out of his destitution in Scotland, and his going to Ulster was motivated first by economic consideration. Also, the trip to Ulster allowed the Scotsman to "go into all the world and preach the Gospel," as Matthew 28:19 enjoined in reference to spreading Christianity. Of course, Ireland at this time was Christian, but according to the Scot, not of the "right kind."

Everything was propitious for a major settlement in Ulster in the early 1600s, and the Lowland Scots were ready to take their part in it. When they got to Ulster, their identification as "Scotch-Irish" expanded.

The Irish Setting: The term "Scotch-Irish"

In a sense, the term "Scotch-Irish" is misleading, even stereotypical, because it implies that only immigrants from the Scottish Lowlands populated Ulster. Just like the "Holy Roman Empire," which was not "holy," "Roman," nor particularly an "Empire," "Scotch-Irish" is an inaccurate term for Ulster settlers, who included Puritans from England, Huguenots from France, and refugees from Holland, as well as Lowlanders from Scotland. The latter group was the most numerous, which set them off from all the others, and encouraged the term "Scotch-Irish."

Thomas F. Hudson traces the term to 1573 when Elizabeth, writing about a nobleman named "Sorley Boy," referred to him as one "of the Scotch-Irish race." In 1675, when Francis Makemie (who later immigrated to America) enrolled in the University of Glascow, his enrollment record identified him as *Scoto-Hibernicus*. In 1723, in New Castle, Delaware, the minister of the Church of England complained about the obstinancy of the "Scotch-Irish."[31]

Some authorities on the Scotch-Irish, however, say the name came into general use this way: When the immigrations were made from Ulster to America starting in the early eighteenth century, all the new arrivals were known in America as "Irish," or "Ulstermen," or "Irish Presbyterians." When in the mid-nineteenth century, floods of Catholics from the south of Ireland came to the United States, the earlier "Ulstermen," being fierce Protestant Presbyterians, wanted to distinguish themselves from the hated Papists. They therefore began to call themselves "Scotch-Irish."[32] Some nineteenth century historians apparently never dropped the practice of equating "Irish" and "Scotch-Irish," arguing that the latter term had often been used to disparage the deeds, heroic and otherwise, of the former. Historian William V. Shannon, however, in his 1963 study of the Irish, took exception to this belief: "Unless one . . . lets the Protestant immigrants from eighteenth century Ireland be denominated as a separate group, the Scotch-Irish, one is forced into the awkward position of identifying a person such as Woodrow Wilson, as 'Irish, which he certainly was not in any sense in which he or his Irish Catholic contemporaries used the term.''[33]

Author Carl Wittke noted, ''That the Scotch-Irish were becoming sensitive about being confused with the Irish is evident from such stray bits of evidence as a protest in 1720 by inhabitants of Londonderry, New Hampshire, who solemnly resolved: 'We were surprised to hear ourselves termed *Irish people* when we so frequently ventured our all for the British Crown and Liberties against the Irish Papists.' ''[34]

William F. Adams, in *Ireland and Irish Emigration to the New World From 1815 to The Famine*, maintained that ''The Scots-Irish peasants of Ulster . . . retained habits and traits which set them apart from the native Irish.[35] And David Doyle argued that ''the first and crucial point to make is that Ulster Irish and native Irish immigrants lived largely separate existences.[36] It seems clear, then, that ''Scotch-Irish'' is different from both ''Scots'' and ''Irish'' in the colonial experiences of British North America.

England's Irish Problem

The ''Irish problem'' for the British dated to the twelfth century, when Henry II invaded Ireland and redistributed its lands to Anglo-Norman families, including four distinct Irish ''kingdoms''; Munster, Leinster, Connaught, and Ulster. This last kingdom contained nine counties,[37] and became of central importance in various English colonization schemes, and ultimately in the colonization of America.

In 1169 a Norman, John de Courcy, with a sizeable army behind him, invaded and conquered Counties Antrim and Down in Ulster. Edward Bruce made numerous incursions from Scotland, situating colonies of Scots in various places.[38] Other of the early colonial entrepreneurs in Ireland included Agnes Campbell and John MacDonnell. These persons, plus many others, were generally encouraged by the English government to plant outposts not only in Ireland but also on the islands between Scotland and Ulster to alleviate what it considered to be an over-population problem.[39]

In addition to these state sanctioned programs, hundreds of individual Scots came on their own, as did many individual Englishmen. England's relationship with Ireland encouraged Scottish mercenaries to join with one group or another and help subdue local populations. The passage of stolen goods and criminals just one step ahead of the law was commonplace between Scotland and Ulster.[40] Once in Ulster, these latter knew that not too many questions would be asked about their backgrounds because their presence was valuable.

By the time Henry VIII ascended the throne in 1509, English colonization schemes in Ireland were not as numerous as in previous times.[41] He did not appreciably increase English holdings in Ireland because of his conciliatory policies of "peaceable ways and amiable persuasions."[42] Under the rule of his daughter, Mary (1553–1558), a law was passed forbidding all Scots to enter Ireland. Mary, a Papist, did not want any troublesome Scottish Presbyterians upsetting the Catholic dominance of Ireland. In addition, it was made a felony—again with the intention of preventing any changes in Irish Catholicism—for Englishmen to intermarry with the Irish.[43] Mary empowered the Earl of Sussex to make certain incursions into Ulster; however, the war with France occupied most of Mary's time and she never gave full authority for military actions against the various factions in north Ireland. She died in 1558, and soon thereafter the Treaty of Cateau-Cambresis was formulated, ending the war with France and diminishing much of the "Scoto-Irish" problem,[44] a situation that held true for only a brief period.

Elizabeth and Ireland

At the beginning of Elizabeth's reign in 1558, she did not seem to be interested in pursuing the Ulster question. She told Sussex that "she had no money for such expensive plans" (that is, for militarily subduing north Ireland), and it would suit her better if she could come to terms with the Scots in Ulster "on the understanding that they would settle down as loyal subjects."[45]

As Elizabeth's reign progressed, however, she became thoroughly concerned about developments in Ulster. For one thing, Scotland and the Ulster Gaels returned to an alignment with France. No Tudor monarch, certainly not Elizabeth, could treat any such concert with anything less than hostility, for France was England's traditional enemy.

Moreover, as a part of her sense of realpolitik, Elizabeth became the champion of Protestantism in Europe; wherever she found a chance of establishing a Protestant foothold, she took it. (The Catholic Church did not consider Elizabeth to be legitimate, since she was the daughter of Henry VIII and his second wife, Anne Boleyn, whom Henry married after divorcing Catherine of Aragon). She became interested in taming the "Wild Irish," and making them loyal *Protestant* subjects of England.

Thus, she listened to the advice of people like Sir Henry Sidney, who wanted to deal militarily with Ireland. In 1567, Sir Henry proposed to secure Ulster by a network of forts and settlements[46] along the coast from Carrickfergus to the mouth of the River Bann.[47] All this accomplished, Sidney suggested that 2,000 "good and dutiful" English subjects to Queen Elizabeth be planted in Ulster. They would farm the area, fish the waters, pay taxes and rent, and yield an annual profit of £5,000 to the crown.[48]

It was not so much that Sidney's proposal was too visionary as that it became lost in bureaucratic tangles. Elizabeth's chief advisor, Lord Cecil, while not dismissing it altogether, said ambiguously that Sidney's plan for settling Ulster was "better liked than thought likely to be obtained."[49] Also, other people such as Thomas Chatterton, Nicholas Malby, and Sir Thomas Smith (Elizabeth's principal secretary) made various proposals to the Queen that caused her to neglect and then ignore Sidney's ideas. Chatterton wanted to limit the years by which an Irishman and Scotsman obtained land leases in Ulster,

Malby proposed to settle lands in County Down, and Sir Thomas Smith and his son wished to colonize the Ardes in County Down and Upper Clandeboy in Antrim.[50]

The Smith efforts at Irish colonization earned the ire of Sir Brian mac Phelim O'Neill, who thought of the Smiths as encroachers. The result was bad blood between Smith and O'Neill, which culminated in the latter's burning of Carrickfergus. News of Carrickfergus's near destruction caused a sensation in England, and led many people to ponder the English presence in Ireland.[51]

The Carrickfergus incident inspired a young man named Walter Devereaux, better known as the Earl of Essex, to formulate a plan to settle the "Irish problem" once and for all.[52] In May, 1573, he proposed a joint venture between himself and Elizabeth. They would share alike in the expenses, and he, Essex, would invade Ireland with 1,200 men, and as many "gentlemen adventurers" as he could find.[53]

The Essex expedition fared no better than previous ones. A storm scattered his force between Liverpool and Belfast; many of his men deserted and went back to England, and Elizabeth wavered in her support. Essex finally offered to cede responsibility for his part in the expedition solely to Elizabeth, so Ireland could be shown as a national problem rather than one of individual undertakings.[54]

Two powerful Irish earls, Tyrone and Tyrconnell, formed a "grand alliance"[55] against the English in 1595. They were confronted by Sir Charles Blount Mountjoy, and especially by Sir Arthur Chichester, considered by many historians to be a principal founder of Ulster's major city, Belfast.[56]

The Work of Arthur Chichester

Chichester, appointed as England's Lord Deputy for Ireland in 1603, received tracts of land in Antrim, and he sponsored many farmers from Devon as settlers.[57] He seemed to have been more successful at native pacification than previous invaders like Sussex and Essex. Chichester wrote to the Governor of Carrickfergus in 1606 about the need to control certain lawless elements who had committed murders and spoils in Ulster. He authorized the sheriff to raise a number of men, divide them into small parties, give them one month's rations, and send them after the malefactors. These posses were authorized to cross county lines in the pursuit of the criminals, but were specifically commanded not to "oppress or exact anything" from the local populace except "necessary assistance."[58]

Also, Chichester became adept at preventing troubles, rather than having to deal with them once they started. For example, word came to Chichester that one O'Cahan was putting "abusive buzzes" into the heads of his tenants against the English. Chichester therefore ordered the Sheriff of Coleraine to invest O'Cahan's castle with a force of some two hundred men. Furthermore, Chichester ordered that O'Cahan's tenants be kept in the place of their present abode, and not allowed to secret themselves "into woods nor fastnesses or remote or solitary places."[59] He obviously wanted to keep an eye on these tenants, and keep them from spreading mischief.

Whereas previous representatives of the Crown, like Mountjoy, had pursued a "scorched earth" policy dealing with the Irish, Chichester used a combination of forebearance, punishments, and preventive actions. He tended, too, to punish only the offenders, rather than making entire populations the victims of his punitive actions. These habits helped to calm tensions in the countryside and lessened the power and influence of the Irish nobles.

In addition to facing their largely losing battles with Chichester, the Irish nobles now heard of another troubling prospect. When Queen Elizabeth died on 24 March 1603, her successor was James VI of Scotland who became James I of England. Disquieting reports had it that James's principal minister, Sir Francis Bacon, had plans for inundating Ulster with people from the Scottish Lowlands, believing they would surpass, or at least neutralize, Irish influences. It was widely held that James, being a Scotsman himself, might be successful in transplanting his own countrymen, particularly to such a short distance away in northern Ireland.

The dismal prospects of subjugation by Chichester and replacement by Scottish Lowlanders prompted many Irish noblemen to leave the country. In fact, 1607 is known as the year of the "Flight of the Earls." Headed by Tyrone and Tyrconnell, about one hundred Gaelic chieftains and their followers left Lough Swilley in north Donegal to go into exile in Europe. Of course their lands, some half million acres in Tyrone, Tyrconnell, and Fermanagh, were confiscated.[60] Many Irish nobles remained, some voluntarily ceding their lands to the Crown, hoping this submissiveness would cause the king to re-grant their properties to them; as it turned out, this was a forlorn objective in most instances.

Chichester's power and influence grew, in large part because of the Flight of the Earls. In July 1608, the deputies and commissioners of Armagh wrote to him that the leaders of every sept (divisions of a clan) had been ordered to deliver the names of all their kinsmen and others who lived under their authority to the sheriffs of each county, and that these names be recorded in a book, and renewed from time to time.[61] This periodical census–taking, it was hoped, would enable the English authorities to monitor the activities of the household heads in each of the counties. However, as the Lord Deputy of Armagh wrote to Chichester (on the same day as did the Armagh commissioners):

> The most part of the inhabitants of this country [Ireland] do not live together in villages and townships after the manner of His Majesty's civil subjects in other parts of this Kingdom, but do all the summer season pass from place to place grazing their . . . heards of cattle, having no other houses or dwellings but only sleight cabbanes . . . not placing them together in the form of a town but scattering and single . . . thereby does arise daily many mischiefs.[62]

This movement of flocks and herds by the Irish came later to be known as "transhumance," a practice of establishing summer encampments in pastures and other rural areas while the oats were growing. David Beers Quinn pointed out that during such movements, "settlement was concentrated not in towns or large villages but either in small irregular rural units or in individual farmsteads."[63]

The "loose and unsettled manner of living" by the Irish encouraged highwaymen, because there could be no hue and cry after them; it also made it almost impossible for a sheriff to serve a warrant and difficult to create trade and handicrafts among the populace.[64] If all these people could be gathered together in villages and towns, asserted the Lord Deputy, they would be "reduced" to a "more civil manner of living," and would grow to "greater wealth and riches."[65] And, he hinted, if the English government could not persuade the "wild Irish" through either sweet reason or force to settle down, then perhaps some other peoples such as the Scottish Lowlanders might be enticed to take their place.

All the conditions seemed to be right for the Crown to think about the possibility of creating an "Ulster Plantation," including the continuing neutralization of the Irish nobles and an increasing determination by Chichester and other representatives of the English government to create towns and communities in Ulster. Furthermore, a Scotsman on the throne undoubtedly had great influence on the attitudes and opinions of his countrymen toward colonization.

Following five centuries of English and Scottish incursions into Ulster, the Lowland Scot migration was far from an isolated event. Rather, the Lowlanders were the last, albeit the most successful, settlers.

The Beginnings of the Ulster Plantation

The Ulster Plantation should be viewed in the context of a large, general colonization program enacted during the early Stuart period. Jamestown, Virginia, the first permanent English colony in North America, was settled in 1607, just as "immigration fever" for Ulster infected the Ulster Scots.

(England was also establishing colonies in the West Indies during this general period, turning "outward" after its defeat of the Spanish Armada in 1588.) The great motive for colonizing Virginia was economic; almost everybody who went to Jamestown expected to profit from it. While the economic motive was strong in Ulster, religious and military objectives also prevailed. At the time of the migrations to Ulster, the Lowlands were "hotbeds of religious enthusiasm."[66] Many Lowlanders, quite apart from any economic gains they expected in Ulster, migrated for the express purpose of spreading their religion.[67] Also, from a military viewpoint, England's requisition of Ulster was a blow against its traditional enemy, France. Sir Arthur Chichester believed that James could better influence history "by pacifying Ireland and replenishing it with 'civil men' " than by recovering any of the French territories that once belonged to England.[68]

The Ulster Plantation began through a system of "undertakers," men of affairs in Scotland and England, who agreed to swear an oath of supremacy to the king, live in Ulster for at least five years and entice an appropriate number of Scotsmen and Englishmen to their holdings.[69] There were six counties of the Plantation: Donegal and Tyrone were primarily Scottish in settlement, Armagh and Derry were English, and Fermanagh and Cavan were mixed with both English and Scottish settlers.[70]

The crown utilized an hierarchical scheme of land grants in Ulster. The king granted a holding to an undertaker who could then lease it to persons of lesser stature who, in turn, could sublease to tenants. Of course, many private individuals in the past had taken land grants unto themselves, but under the operation of the Ulster program in the early 1600s, they were vulnerable to the king's authority. For example, Sir Cahir O'Dougherty, an Irish landholder, rebelled against the king in 1608, and for his troubles lost all of his holdings—the entire county of Coleraine—which were subsequently added to the Ulster properties. O'Dougherty's defeat encouraged James to speed up his conquest of Ireland,[71] and also began the English practice of sending Scottish troops for foreign conquest.[72] By about 1610, seventy-seven Scottish and English undertakers controlled some 81,000 acres in Ulster.[73] A rent of £ 5 6s and 8d for each 1,000 acres was to be paid annually to the king.[74]

James received much support for his Ulster colony from the merchant guilds in England.[75] Twelve London companies received major portions of County Coleraine, and then changed its name to Londonderry.[76] James got help from varying levels of Lowland Scot society. Some authors maintain that the Ulster-bound Scot was of the "highest character," leaving home to benefit his family and to spread the Presbyterian creed.[77] Others claim that Ulster attracted the "scum of both nations" of Scotland and England, and that going to Ireland "was a miserable mark of a deplorable person."[78] As is almost always the case, the truth about the character of those settlers in Ulster was that they were neither saint nor sinner, but a hodge-podge of people with different values and ethical concerns.

Growth of Colonization

Colonization programs depend in part, at least, on a push-pull effect; a push from the old country, and a pull from the new one. Conditions in Lowland Scotland in the sixteenth and seventeenth centuries provided some pushes. Once the first wave of settlement occurred in Ulster and reports were sent back home about the fertility of the soil, protection from hostile forces (each undertaker was required to build forts of various kinds), and living in settled communities, there were some pulls.

The parallels between the Ulster and Jamestown colonizations are striking. After the first rush of enthusiasm in both places, bad luck and periods of lethargy set in. In 1610–11, Jamestown had its "starving time," and in 1614–15, Ulster suffered its "killer winter," when cattle died in the snow and people had little or nothing to eat.[79] In the 1620s Jamestown endured a series of disastrous Indian wars; the greatest danger to the Scots in their new land was the displaced natives, some of whom vowed eternal vengeance against the interlopers. (It has frequently been asserted that when the Scotch-Irish got to America, they already had much experience in disfranchising those who got there before them.) Whenever each colony began to show signs of unusual industry and economic entrepreneurship (Jamestown with tobacco and naval stores, Ulster with linen products and grain), the English government quickly asserted its control over the two provinces through regulations and tariffs. Most Englishmen who expressed themselves on colonization preferred Ulster to Virginia (though by 1613, one of the Ulster settlements in County Cavan was named "Virginia").[80] Conditions in Ulster were merely "difficult," while those in Virginia were "disastrous." As Sir Arthur Chichester said: "I had rather labour with my hands in the plantation of Ulster than dance or play in that of Virginia."[81]

As for the number of people who settled the Ulster Plantation, only a few hundred came to start with, and some of them returned to Scotland during the first year. According to Scotch-Irish authority M. Perceval-Maxwell, there were four categories of Scottish settlers in Ulster: freeholders, who held the largest leases after the undertakers; leaseholders and cottagers, common folk who lived in Ulster just about the way they had in Scotland; artisans, masons, and builders, whose services were sorely needed; and finally, ministers.[82] The latter were brought as a continuing commitment of the Scotsman to his Presbyterianism and his desire to convert the "heathen" Irish.

Another expert on the Scotch-Irish, Philip Robinson, asserted that in 1619 there were 126 castles and 1,897 dwelling houses made of stone and timber "after the English manner."[83] In the fall of 1611, the Scottish population in the Ulster counties that had fallen to the Crown was estimated at between 350 and 700 adults.[84] By 1622 this number had grown some tenfold. These were the persons whose descendants ultimately migrated to America, and formed the people known to the world as the "Scotch-Irish."

Nature of King James I

Why was James I, crotchety in personality and largely unloved by his subjects, successful in colonizing Ulster while previous, more popular monarchs such as Elizabeth I were not? While James was not more ardent than his predecessors in displacing Roman Catholicism in Ireland and replacing it with Protestants, he was more pragmatic than previous monarchs. Certainly a sign of his pragmatism was his earlier reaction to the execution of his mother, Mary, Queen of Scots, by Elizabeth. James was aware as he was growing up that Elizabeth was the last of the Tudors, and that he, through his father, the Earl of Darnley, had an excellent chance of being the first monarch to reign over both Scotland and England. Thus, when Mary was beheaded at Fotheringay Castle, James limited himself to a protest, and a rather mild one at that, for he did not want to jeopardize his own personal safety or his chances at the throne of England.

When he did assume the English Crown, he took up the "Irish Question" where Elizabeth had left it. He thought about bringing in settlers from Holland or perhaps Germany to displace the troublesome Irish Catholics, whom he even thought about sending to America to get them out of Europe altogether. It was probably Sir Francis Bacon who turned James's attention toward his own countrymen, the Scots, for purposes of colonization.

Sir Francis, purposefully excluding the Highland Scot, recommended the Lowland Scot to be central to the Ulster Plantation. The Highlander was too intractable, too unyielding in his ways and personality. The Lowlander was difficult enough, but he was an admixture of nationalities, and the influences of the English were greatest on him. Thus, Bacon believed, he seemed the most likely individual to bring James's plans to fruition.

A report written sometime around 1611 justified the royal initiatives in Ulster. The Irish, it was said, had "yielded to peace," and there is now "little noise among them." In the past the Irish had wanted only to be "rich" in men and arms, but since the Scottish colonization by James I, they strove "to lay hold of a resting place" for their posterity. The report concluded (too optimistically, as it turned out) that the "title of 'conquered nation' will soon be forgotten [among the Irish]," and they would become loyal, law-abiding citizens of the English realm.[85]

Difficulties After James

Despite the bad winter of 1614–1615, the Ulster colony grew while James was on the throne. Just after his death in 1625, migration from Scotland slowed to a trickle. James's successor, his son Charles I, did not seem overly interested, at least at the beginning of his reign, in the Irish problem. Then, in the 1630s, immigration began anew, and once more hundreds of Lowland Scots made their ways to northern Ireland.

There was a new round of bad harvests in the Lowlands in the early 1630s, and rents increased. Additionally, civil strife became a constant reality in the Lowlands, especially along the border between Scotland and England. Under James, a border police force had been created to stop contraband from passing between the two countries and to halt the incessant feuds among the landholders, or lairds. Innocent bystanders were frequently caught up in the warfare and became its victims. Such conditions in Scotland provided another push for the Lowlander to take his family on the short trip across the sea to Ulster and start a new life.

The most persistent incentive for renewed immigration was religion. Some authors like Philip Robinson assert that "although Presbyterianism was a dominant philosophy" among the Lowlanders, it was not "a distinct religious denomination until the late 17th century."[86] Whatever the case, it was clear that the Lowland Scot's religious ideal came to differ from that held by the majority of Englishmen. Although by birth James was Presbyterian, he became "low-church" Anglican, with little stress on ritual or general authority of bishops. (While it is true that the crowns of England and Scotland through James were united, both countries retained their separate political identities during his reign). Anglicanism figured in James's plans for the Ulster Plantation, but he was practical enough not to force any strong compliance by the Lowland Protestants to the Anglican form of Christianity. He apparently realized that his plan of neutralizing Catholic Ireland would go astray if he got bogged down in the religious differences between the Scots and the formalities of the Church of England. The Presbyterian Scot believed in original sin, predestination, and a personal relationship with God. At least under James, so did many of the Anglicans. While he was in power, Ulster was covered by the Anglican Church of Ireland, which accepted predestination. Indeed, the Primate of the Church of Ireland appointed by James, Archbishop Ussher, was a Calvinist in his theology. Anglicanism, however, became ritualized, especially when the "high-church" party came to power under Charles I, and in time, many Scotsmen came to see little difference between Anglicanism and Roman Catholicism.

James's accommodating attitude toward the Presbyterian Scots did not continue under Charles, who seemed not to possess any of the pragmatic qualities of his father. As Wallace Notestein pointed out, "Charles had no sense of the possible, nor any understanding of the Scots."[87] Both Charles and William Laud, Archbishop of Canterbury, chose Anglican conformity rather than any system of religious liberality. Landowners were required to swear their loyalty to King Charles and the established Church, and hundreds of Scotsmen left to get away from these religious strictures.

Laud's zeal for religious conformity soon spread to Ireland, and the migrating Scots once again found themselves in the quagmire of religious controversy. A climax of sorts occurred in 1641 when Laud and the Lord Deputy of Ireland, Thomas Wentworth (Lord Strafford), imposed upon the Scottish inhabitants of Ireland the so-called "Black Oath," in which they were required to show their fealty to king and church. It read in part:

> I do faithfully swear, profess, and promise, that I will honor and obey my Sovereign, Lord King Charles, and bear fruitful and true allegiance to him. . . . And that I will not bear arms or do any rebellious or hostile act against him or protest against any of His Majesty's royal commands. . . . I do renounce and abjure all covenants, bonds, oaths, whatsoever contrary to what I have sworn herein, professed and promised, so help me God in Christ.[88]

Ulster Scots, on pain of fines and forfeiture of lands, had to take this oath that the English claimed was "vulgarly" called the "Black Oath."[89] This Black Oath was the start of a long process that led thousands of Ulster Scots to the decision to go to America.

Conformity to the standards of the Anglican Church and the English Parliament's increasing concern that some of Ulster's products such as linen and grains would put manufacturers in England at a competitive disadvantage began to work against the Scots in Ulster as early as the 1640s. As time passed, and especially in the middle to late eighteenth century, when Parliament seemed to have a "death wish" vis-a-vis its colonies not only in Ulster but America as well, tariffs and export duties rose on colonial products, sometimes to prohibitive levels.

Unyielding hostility from the native Irish constituted the greatest problem for seventeenth century Ulster Scots. Today, in the closing years of the twentieth century, Ulster is a near-perfect historical laboratory, where the results of the policies of James I can be seen on the sidewalks and streets of Coleraine, Londonderry, and Belfast. The rank bitterness and enmity between Catholics and Protestants in Northern Ireland today date essentially from James's Ulster Plantation.

Many writers have attributed an aspect of permanency to the Ulster Scots, arguing that they would have stayed indefinitely in north Ireland if religious and economic hardships had not developed. It would probably have been uncharacteristic of the Lowland Scots as a whole, however, to think in terms of permanency after they had made the trip to Ireland. The

Lowlander had long been a "mover," if not to take part in various European wars, then to relocate to different places within his own country to get enough fertile land for crops and wood for fire. If conditions had remained ideal or even good in Ulster, many a Scotsman would still have moved on. Later, this mobility became a well-known American characteristic. Eminent historian Richard Hofstadter claimed that American pioneers were not so much interested in permanent settlement as in buying property, improving it for some years, selling it for a profit, and then "moving on."[90]

The vastness of the North American environment transformed European immigrants accustomed to dealing with small lease-holds and idealistic European philosophies, and created Americans who were the products both of Old World sentiments and New World frontier realities. The Scotch-Irish joined other immigrant groups in creating this system of American practicality.

CHAPTER TWO

The Deepening "Irish Problem"

Nature of Colonization

After the Lowland Scots had lived in Ulster for two generations, were they still Scots or had they become Irish? Or were they now both, or neither? These questions have intrigued historians and sociologists for years. One might also ask: After the first generation at Jamestown, did the people there cease to be English and become Americans?

To try to arrive at answers to these questions is futile. Direct immigrations from Scotland to Ulster and from England to America continued through the seventeenth and eighteenth centuries. Most immigrants in America were American English; in north Ireland, Ulster Scots. They were each the heirs of two different worlds; both were frontiersmen, taking their old ways of life with them, acquiring new ones, and in the process becoming a new people altogether.

Another question of long interest concerns the lack of intermarriage between Ulster Scots and the native Irish. So great was the hatred of the displaced natives toward the Scots that little, if any, social mixing occurred between them. The Ulstermen continually "worried about being attacked by the 'wild Irish' in the hills," and about uprisings of the "tame Irish" in the towns.[1] As a result of these concerns, sales of guns were prohibited to the Irish, along with powder and shot.[2] The hatreds and distrusts kept the Scots and Irish apart; there was some social mingling and intermarriage between the Ulster Scots and French Huguenots and Hollanders, but for the most part, while in the north of Ireland, they maintained their ethnicity.

Their continuing ethnicity in Ulster derived from circumstances rather than philosophy; they did not particularly feel superior to any other people, except perhaps in their religion. The Ulster Scots were frequently described as "humble folks"; yet they carried with them the elitist attitudes regarding the notions of predestination and elect. Once the Ulster Scots got to America, they did not intermarry with the natives, the Indians, but they certainly did with other ethnic groups such as the Dutch, Germans, and French. Some authors have maintained that the Scotch-Irish themselves were no longer a distinct ethnic group directly after the American Revolution. This thesis is, however (see chapter 8), not entirely accurate.

Continuing Religious Problems

It was difficult enough for the Ulster Scots to deal with the "tame" and "wild" Irish, but their religious problems with England grew increasingly worse. To offset the religious offensives of Archbishop Laud, the Presbyterians in Scotland and Ireland made covenants with one another in the late 1630s to resist conformity to the Church of England. Thus began a long, bitter struggle between the established church and dissenters.

The case of Isabel Montgomrie illustrates the bitter relations between the Anglican church and the covenanters. Eight weeks after her husband died, *he* was ordered to appear before the High Commission in Dublin to explain his adherence to the "National Covenant and Confession" of the Kirk of Scotland. Even though the Commission had been informed of

Montgomrie's death, it still levied a fine of £20 against him for his religious persuasions.

When the fine went unpaid, soldiers came to Isabel's house, took away all the cows and horses, and drove her and her eight children twenty miles into the wilderness. When the authorities learned that she, too, was an ardent member of the Kirk, they issued warrants for her arrest, causing her to forsake her children and become a fugitive from the law.

Isabel ultimately petitioned the Earl of Rochester, Governor of Ulster for a redress of grievances, without results. Her petition claimed that she was now separated from her children because of her religious beliefs and was without "all means of sustenation." Her plea gave a remorseful picture of what was happening in Ireland: "[These are] extraordinary hard measures done to me as to many hundreds more of our nation for adherence to our covenant with God. I do in all humility remonstrate to Your Grace . . . entreating that such crying sins of oppression against the widow and the fatherless and many more of this nation may by Your Grace . . . be manifested to the King's Majesty for redress."[3] Montgomrie's petition foreshadowed the future, for the religious situation in Ireland got even worse under the late Stuart king, James II, and caused thousands of Ulstermen to make up their minds to go to America.

Military Problems

The English civil war, 1640–46, deeply affected the Scots living in Ulster. It was not so much a matter of Ulster Scots taking sides between Charles I and Oliver Cromwell as it was of being repressed by one army after another, and being forced to give money and provisions first to one side and then the other as their armies campaigned across Ireland. To complicate matters, a Scottish army was also present, demanding its "dues" from the hapless citizens, and requisitioning most of Belfast as a garrison for its troops.[4]

The native Irish took advantage of the outbreak of the

English civil war and rebelled against the Ulster Scots in 1641. At times it appeared that the Plantation would be overwhelmed, and the settlers killed off. Help came, however, from a Scottish army raised under Lieutenant General George Monroe and, though the country remained in a state of anarchy, the Irish were driven back. When the Royalists were defeated in England in 1646, Oliver Cromwell crossed to Ireland with a Parliamentary army which restored order by crushing the remaining Irish insurgents.

All accounts of the Irish uprising document the horrible events that occurred as Catholic and Protestant flailed each other with furies pent up from many years of mutual hatred. Historians of both religious persuasions blame the other side for the atrocities. William E. H. Lecky wrote that the rebellion stemmed from a mass recollection of the dispossessed, who remembered that Elizabeth starved their parents and James drove them from their inheritances. Women and children, Lecky said, had been "deliberately massacred," and "no quarter had been given to prisoners."[5] Protestant historian Maude Glascow, on the other hand, attributed the Irish uprisings to the Jesuits, arguing that "the atrocities are so dreadful that they cannot appear on the printed page." In Fermanagh, Protestant almost to a person, Glascow asserted that only twenty people escaped the Catholic wrath. The rebels, she reported, "destroyed cattle and sheep, not for food, but because they belonged to the Protestants."[6] Estimates run as high as one-third of the Protestants in Ireland being killed, which would be near the half million mark.[7] No precise figures are available for Catholic casualties, but they were less than those suffered by the Protestants.

The Ulster Scots had to endure not only warfare from the Irish, but also deprivations from visiting armies. A letter of 1645 to the Commissioners of Ulster stated that "the want of power . . . to govern the Army is the cause of many evils."[8] A petition the following year stated that the "pressures under which the poor British inhabitants in Ulster groan" were caused in part by the "exorbitant and unequal . . . levying of taxes by . . . officers and soldiers of the British regiments . . ."[9] If such conditions were not relieved, continued the Ulster petition, all the villages and towns in north Ireland would disappear as their inhabitants fled to the wildernesses to escape the heavy hand of the British armies, thus effectively destroying the Ulster Plantation.

The Ulster Commission issued strict orders that Ulstermen "continually be within some distinct quarters" and stop the newly revived practice of "removing themselves in flocks from one place to another." Having permanent abodes would render less likely the "unequal assessments" of taxes from the British and Scottish armies operating in Ireland.

The Commission paid special attention to the ways in which the Scottish armies carried on their business in Ireland. The Scots recruited their companies and regiments from the civil populace of Ulster, and had apparently raised five bodies of troops in this manner. Local recruiting was a "prejudicial practice to the Crown and contrary to the clear intention of the treaty twixt the two kingdoms [of Scotland and England]."

The British officers were commanded to "give all encouragement to the country people to proceed in ploughing and other husbandry by assuring them of your countenance and protection." Nor would the country people be exposed to the "arbitrary taxacions of the soldiers. . . . Special regard shall be had of them, and they not be oppressed but cherished."[10]

For all these fine promises, the Ulster Commissioners and the English Parliament were not motivated by kindness in ordering the Scottish armies away from Ulster civilians. Their motive, it seems clear, was self interest. If Scotland used Ulstermen as soldiers, then Ulster was rendered "less able to apply such supplies and recruits to the British army."[11] Ulster was there to serve the interests of the English Parliament and any deviation from that course was to be dealt with quickly and firmly.

The Irish uprising continued spasmodically and did not finally end until 1652, leaving an all but prostrate Ireland. Thereafter, many Ulstermen kept themselves heavily armed and formed vigilante groups to act against the Catholics. Some historians have identified Ireland's miseries of the time as a part of a larger picture, one that depicted a denouement between Catholicism and Protestantism after a century of bantering against each other. While religion played a major role in the Irish problem, forcible dispossession of property without proper recompense to create the Ulster Plantation was the main factor.

The age of the Ulster Plantation was one marked by brutal religious wars throughout Europe. While England had been locked into its civil war and the struggle in Ireland, the Thirty Years' War in the German provinces had raged. In 1648 the Thirty Years' War ended with the Peace of Westphalia, in Germany, heralding a period when countries would go to war more for nationalistic than religious reasons. This condition did not hold in Ireland; while it is true that Ulster prospered (at least by comparison with earlier times) under Cromwell and the Restoration King, Charles II, the religious conflict remained, ever ready to rise up and cast doom upon the land.

A Short Period Of Peace

Attaining a stability of sorts after the English civil war and the Irish uprising, the Ulstermen resumed their old ways of life. Their beef industry had been struck an almost fatal blow by the military conflicts,[12] causing them to turn to woolen manufactories, using the "low" or "Dutch" spinning wheels for fine yarns.[13] They also created a lively export trade in barrel staves and animal hides,[14] especially those of wolves, for which they sometimes paid bounties as high as £6 each.[15]

Settling down into permanent villages and towns, long an objective of the English government, increasingly became a reality in Ulster during this period. Houses, churches, and public buildings were erected that were meant to stay. Lime and stone were used for houses occupied by wealthy lords and other influential people. Clay, mud, and wooden posts were the most common materials for an ordinary house, with an open hearth situated in the center.[16] Slate was plentiful in parts of Ireland, and put to good use during the postwar reconstructions, especially as roofs for churches. Despite the assertions about the educational proclivities of Ulstermen, "only a select few of the plantation towns could boast a schoolhouse."[17] Instruction in basic subjects like reading, writing, and arithmetic and, of course, in Protestant Christianity, continued in the homes and churches.

Ulster became so pacified between 1652 and 1670 that it was a haven for persecuted minorities elsewhere. Covenanters from Scotland and Puritans from England arrived in large numbers directly after the restoration of the Stuarts in 1660, as did Quakers. Huguenots from France landed as French moods began to shift against them. (Later, in 1685, the Edict of Nantes was repealed, and Huguenots poured into Ulster by the thousands.) Charles II proved to be not very serious about controlling the Presbyterians in north Ireland, leaving them largely to their own religious proclivities.

Presbyterians Against Other Religions

Some other groups, however, especially the Quakers, presented a problem to the Ulster Presbyterians: their method of worship differed, sometimes sharply, from that of the Scotch covenanters. Thus, the Ulstermen wanted to enact some "conforming" regulations of their own. In addition to maintaining the right to set their own creeds and make rules for appointing their own ministers, they created ecclesiastical courts to deal with heretics and miscreants.

In 1672, for example, Preacher Thomas Wyllie signed an order for the Ballymoney Presbyterians at each of their meetings to appoint a brethren to "gather out" the most dangerous errors found in Quaker pamphlets, and confute them. Anyone friendly to the "black mysteries" of Quakerism, he claimed, was without all "foundation of religion." These "wayfaring" Quakers, the good reverend wrote, had "no call from God," and he insisted that many of them were Jesuit priests in disguise, and therefore "anti-Christ pedlars," preaching to the poor people, "the rotten wares of Rome."[18]

In addition to ferreting out Quakers and Papists from among them, the Ulster Presbyterians also brought many of their constituents to account for "misbehavior." One such was David Houstoune who, as a "licensed probationer" for the ministry, did not wish to take the advice of his presbytery at Ballymoney and refrain from preaching at places other than his own parish. He then added the offense of temper to his other indiscretions. A rent occurred between the members of the congregation, some favoring Houstoune, others supporting the presbytery.[19]

Houstoune preached publicly at Dinnicken and Dirnicken, and "the border betwixt the two," and set up a "lecture and preaching diet" during the week in the parish of McCosquie, despite the presence of a bonafide Presbyterian minister in that place. Thus, Houstoune was an "insolent and contemptuous" usurper who "marred the work of the Lord," and could not long be tolerated. He was hailed before the ecclesiastical court in August 1671, and repented for "fixing tent against tent." He regretted that his actions had permitted those opposed to Protestantism to be confirmed in their own minds that Presbyterianism amounted to religious anarchy.[20]

It did not take long for Houstoune to backslide, for in March 1672, he was again cited for contempt of the "good order and restraints" of the Presbyterian hierarchy. This time he did not receive merely a remonstrance; he was expelled from the Balleymoney congregation altogether and stripped of his incipient ministerial position. The people of Balleymoney and Coleraine were advised not to hear him. Apparently these actions halted any preacher's career Houstoune had in mind, for nothing more was heard of him.[21]

The ecclesiastical courts established by the Presbyterians in Scotland and then in north Ireland were part of the cultural and religious baggage they brought with them to America. Throughout Pennsylvania and the other colonies where the Scotch-Irish settled, church courts were a major fact of life. These tribunals looked into the deeds and "misdeeds" of regular members, forcing them to admit their guilt publicly before the entire congregation, an excruciating, sometimes terrifying, experience. One certainly must not attribute any ideas of religious leniency or even freedom to the Scotch-Irish. They were unwavering in their religious requirements and quite intolerant of differing philosophies.

Renewed Troubles Under James II

In 1685 James II ascended the throne of England, and the relatively peaceful state that had fallen on Ulster halted. James was anti-Protestant, with every intention of forcing the Ulster Scots into submission to his will and to the creeds of the Roman Catholic Church. Like his father, Charles I, but definitely unlike his grandfather, James I, James II did not possess the practical qualities necessary to rule over a diverse kingdom; in fact, his lack of common sense ultimately cost him the throne itself.

In 1688, William of Orange landed in England during the "Glorious Revolution," and James fled to France. A year later, James, leading a French army, sought to regain his throne via Ireland. The Ulstermen fled the countryside in the face of James's advance; his scorched earth policy was pursued to such an extent that one French diarist noted that parts of Ulster were like "Arabian deserts."[22]

The Ulstermen left their villages and headed for fortified towns. One such was Londonderry on the River Foyle where, in 1689 James's army laid siege to the Protestants, an event that is still hailed in Scotch-Irish song and poetry. For 105 days, with a watchword of "no surrender," the Ulster Presbyterians held out in the besieged town.[23] Then, in mid-1690, William of Orange came to their rescue. The Battle of the Boyne was fought June 30–July 1, 1690, and in it, James was thoroughly defeated and forced to flee back to France.[24]

Continued Religious Problems

Religious freedom was at least legally offered to the Ulstermen during the reign of William and Mary, and for a decade after the Battle of the Boyne, Ulster Presbyterianism flourished. They prospered so much that the Bishop of Down of the Church of Ireland (Anglican) complained that they exercised jurisdiction "with a high hand over those of their own persuasion." Though an earlier "Act of Uniformity" (1662) cast doubts on the legal rights of children begotten of Presbyterian marriages, "they generally everywhere celebrate the office of matrimony."[25]

The Bishop complained, too, that the Ulster Presbyterians celebrated the Lord's Supper "in congregations formidably numerous" by gathering the inhabitants of ten or twelve or more parishes together in one place. Then they preached in the fields and "continue there a great part of the day together." Also, the Presbyterians set up "philosophical schools" in various places in contempt of the law. If these practices were not curbed, the Bishop of Down asserted, the priests of the established church would be "extremely discouraged" in reclaiming those of "erroneous" ways.[26]

Some of the problems addressed by the Bishop of Down reflected continuing struggles between Presbyterianism and the Anglican Church. It was one thing for Parliament in far away London to grant a few religious freedoms; it was another thing altogether for those freedoms to be practiced without fear of retribution. When the Irish Presbyterians met in the field, as mentioned in the Bishop's complaint, they used a safety device that had begun in Scotland. They all stood in a great circle out in the field, and when the minister started the services, every member of the congregation turned his back on him to spot any authorities of the established church on their way to break up the meeting.[27] This practice the Scotch-Irish brought with them to America, where it was used to herald the presence of any unfriendly Indians.

About 1690, the Presbyterians spelled out their troubles with the established church in a long memorial. Though admittedly they were religious dissenters, their loyalty to the Crown had never faltered. The uncertainties surrounding the legitimacy of Presbyterian marriages bothered them the most, for it left them open to the "damnable" sin of fornication, and to the bastardization of their children. There had been no trouble in the past with these matters; only now in the last decade of the seventeenth century had it cropped up. The authorities should consider "how grievous it may be to a great part of His Majesty's subjects if all marriages not solemnized according to the rites of the established church should be declared void."[28] It was not only Presbyterians who suffered from this unwise policy, but Quakers and Catholics, too. What would be the status of those who conformed to the established church but who had descended from Presbyterians, Quakers, and Catholics? The Presbyterians earnestly beseeched Parliament for an Act of Toleration for all those creeds outside the realm of Anglicanism.

Worsening Religious Conditions

Not only did the Parliament not grant such an Act; it made matters even worse. Queen Anne, the last of the Stuarts, took the throne in 1702; unfortunately, she lent an ear to high church zealots, who were unwilling or unable to learn any lessons from the past. They pushed through the Test Act in Parliament in 1703, which required that all office holders in Ireland use sacraments as prescribed by the established church.[29] As one historian put it, the effect of the Test Act "was to sweep Presbyterian officials out of their posts and Presbyterian ministers out of their pulpits. In one disastrous move the Crown alienated a once loyal people beyond redemption."[30]

The Presbyterians claimed that when the idea of a Test Act first arose, it was designed as a bar against Papists, "whose principles and consciences obliged them to disturb and undermine every government that is not subject to the Pope."[31] Presumably the Presbyterians did not object to Catholics being disfranchised, but when the Test Act swept them in as well, they certainly did protest.

A Presbyterian minister, William Bigger, became involved in the workings of the Test Act when he preached in the town of Drogheda on 3 October 1708. Two days later the Archbishop of Armagh complained to Will Patoun, the town's mayor, and Patoun issued a warrant for Bigger's arrest. The charge was illegal preaching; even the arrest warrant certified that Bigger's sermon was not false doctrine or, worse yet, sedition. It was the fact that his credentials did not come from the Anglican Church that had gotten him into trouble.[32] He ultimately served a short imprisonment for his infraction of the laws.

Bigger's case attracted a great deal of attention and brought sharp protests from every Presbyterian quarter in Ulster. Two "Popish priests" were settled in Drogheda, and they went about their business unmolested, and "dissenting preachers" were permitted to do their work in Dublin. Therefore, why choose Drogheda as a place to enforce the Test Act? The inconsistency of enforcement of the Act, the Ulster Presbyterians maintained, bordered on hypocrisy.

The Presbyterians asserted that they were the largest body of Protestants in Ireland and that they could, "without letting the plough stand," bring 20,000 soldiers to the defense of the realm. The very people in the English Parliament who persecuted them by the Test Act, they warned, should bear in mind that without the Ulster Presbyterians, England's hold against the Catholics "and other foreign powers," would indeed be tenuous.[33]

The big question in the Presbyterians' minds was: Why? They had enjoyed long spells of toleration from the established church, in which they had exercised their religion without governmental restraint. Also, the Ulster Presbyterians had been true and faithful to the Crown. Why should the Parliament now single out the Presbyterians and jail them for disagreeing with the established church? They registered surprise, hurt, and anger at the Test Act.[34]

For their part, however, the agents of the Irish (Anglican) Church defended their actions. Narcissus, the Archbishop of Armagh, maintained that Drogheda had hosted no regular Presbyterian congregation for twenty-eight years. Bigger's sermon was deliberately provocative, designed to show his contempt for the law of the realm; it had disturbed the peace in the otherwise quiet town of Drogheda, and therefore warranted official attention. Furthermore, said the Archbishop, no "dissenters" in Ireland, north or south, had been disturbed, even with the Test Act, if they had a settled congregation.

Narcissus had a few complaints of his own. The Presbyterians had styled the official religion as anti-scriptural, superstitious, and idolatrous. "Our ministers have been openly and violently assaulted and hindered in the discharge of their sacred offices."[35] Even so, the Anglicans, said Narcissus, had not been revengeful: "Amidst these many and repeated provocations we have still been easy and have endeavored by gentle usage to melt them down into a more soft and complying temper, but all our attempts of this kind have proved unsuccessful. They have returned us evil for good. Our forebearance hath only increased their rage and obstinancy."[36]

Moreover, continued the Archbishop, the Ulster Presbyterians had become proselytical: "[N]ot content with the enjoyment of the free exercise of their religious worship and places where they had settled members . . . [they] have assumed the power to send out missionaries to several places of their kingdom [Ireland] where they have no call or any congregation to support them." They had even misused their pension funds from Parliament, claimed the Archbishop. Instead of saving the annual £1200 for the upkeep of retired ministers, they "employed and maintained" agents to create schisms in the established church and used pension money for lawsuits and to form seminaries "to the poisoning of the principles of our youth."[37]

Such charges and countercharges indicated that an incurable breach had occurred between Ulster Presbyterianism and the established Anglican Church. The fluctuations in the two churches' relationships over the years had become increasingly troublesome to the Ulstermen. Under the founder of the Ulster Plantation, James I, freedom of religious practicc was all but assured. Then, Charles I allowed Archbishop Laud and the Earl of Strafford to negate these earlier privileges. The Cromwellian age brought back several measures of relief, and although Parliament passed the Act of Uniformity during the reign of Charles II over the monarch's objections, this era of tolerance continued into the early Restoration period. James II, however, sought to reclaim his whole kingdom for Roman Catholicism, and in the process lost it all. While he was on the throne, he inflicted great miseries upon the citizens of Ulster, whose grandparents had come over from Lowland Scotland. Under William and Mary, religious leniency once again became the order of the day, only to give way to the policies of hard-nosed reactionaries when Queen Anne came to power.

With all these variations, how could the Ulster Presbyterians develop and maintain any sense of permanency? They literally did not know from one year to the next just how their religious practices would be viewed by the state, and they became inured to policies of inconsistency. They got used to mobilizing quickly for any crisis that came their way, and as soon as the crisis dissipated, demobilizing. Later, this practice characterized the American military: to create a force for immediate local defense, and once that objective was obtained, to dismantle that force. The Scotch-Irish did not invent the system of being opposed to standing armies—if anyone did, it was the English. The Ulster Scots, however, accepted the principle and, with the other immigrant groups to America, practiced it on the North American continent.

Economic Problems

Religion apart, the economic relations between Ulster and Parliament produced some traumatic experiences of their own. Slowly, but with an accelerating force, economic sanctions were placed on Ulstermen. And they were placed because of Ulster's success; rarely will one find an economically dissolute entity being controlled or punished through taxes, tariffs, or trade regulation. It is middle class success that breeds such things. While it seems paradoxical that ingenuity and thrift should be repaid with vicious controls, the truth was that Ulster's success endangered the economic interests of many

English merchants who had great influence with the Parliament.

The first major restriction was the Staple Act of 1663, by which Irish products except food, horses, and indentured servants were prohibited from all the other English colonies.[38] This Act cut deeply into the developing woolen industry that had replaced beef production when the latter was largely ruined by the wars and conflicts of the 1640s. Then in 1671, as a further symbol of its control over Ireland, the English Parliament strengthened the rules by which goods could be imported into Ulster.[39] In many instances, there could be no direct importations because of the system of mercantilism employed by the British government. Under mercantilism, colonial products such as wool, American cotton and naval stores and the like had to be sent to England instead of being sold directly to whomever would buy them. Mercantilism worked against the internal economic interests of farmers and merchants both in Ulster and America, and in its process awakened many nerves of protest.

A lengthy recommendation was made in 1697 by the Commissioners of Trade and Plantations to establish and maintain a linen industry in Ulster. Among its suggestions was a "linen school," which all children between six and fourteen who came from poor families would be required to attend.[40] Though no child would be obliged to go above two miles to such a school, he would, while there, work ten hours a day, "or as long as it is light." He would be paid, "according to the ordinary [spinning] rates paid to others," but anything he had spoiled in learning his craft would be deducted. Any parent who did not send his children to the spinning schools would have to deliver to the authorities a quantity of cloth and thread.

Each successful graduate of the spinning schools would be presented with a new wheel for personal use. Spinning competitions for females were to be held in sizeable towns, usually on market day, and the woman who won would get £10 as an award, and her husband would not be required to serve on juries or hold political office.[41] Through the spinning schools, which lasted throughout the eighteenth century,[42] and other efforts, the English Parliament made it clear that it intended to have Ulster for its own exclusive benefits.

In 1699, the Woollens Act was passed, striking an all but fatal blow to the livelihoods of thousands of Ulstermen. Irish wool could not be sold anywhere under the Act except in England and Wales. The Act excluded Ulster from the lucrative continental market, leaving it all to the wool merchants from England. Thousands of Ulstermen went from middle class prosperity to abject poverty with one stroke of the royal pen.

Then came the rent controversy. In 1607, when the Ulster Plantation was officially formed, a one hundred year ban on raising rents was imposed on the undertakers although leases were usually good for only thirty-one years. This policy provided incentives for people to come over from the Lowlands, and once in Ulster, to stay.[43] A century later this ban expired, and the descendants of those first undertakers and others who had become landlords raised rents, which were generally one pence per acre, with a vengeance.[44] The Ulster Scots felt betrayed; they had worked and improved the land considerably, and now for their industry were being penalized with rents four and five times what they had been paying. Many simply refused to pay these new charges, which they considered to be exorbitant.

They probably could have afforded to pay the new rents, but it was the principle of the thing that mattered to them, coupled to a very stubborn pride. Nonetheless, some Ulstermen swallowed their pride, and paid the new rents. Thousands did not, and as a result, they either remained in Ireland as peasants, went to Scotland, the home of their ancestors; or boarded a ship at Belfast or Larne and made the treacherous crossing of the Atlantic to America.

Adding to the man-made miseries, numerous natural calamities also beset the Ulstermen. From 1714 through 1721 disastrous dry seasons took their toll of animals and food crops, causing prices to soar.[45] During this same time, killer frosts occurred in the winters, and cattle and sheep came down with various diseases that all too often proved fatal.[46]

In the face of all these problems, the wonder is not that thousands of Scotch-Irish immigrated, but rather that it took them so long to make up their minds to do it. By the early eighteenth century, they were a long-suffering people, living under the heavy hand of the Anglican Church, the greedy ambitions of mercantilistic-oriented English businessmen, and a Crown that seemed unable to resist the same authoritarian impulses that had gotten the throne into so much trouble in the past.

The push of these difficulties was accompanied by the pull of America. There had been a trickle of Scotch-Irish immigration in the seventeenth century and enough reports sent home for Ulstermen to know that the most available commodity in America was land. Even if a person had to indenture himself to someone for ship passage, he knew he would ultimately become a landowner. If there has ever been such a thing as the "Great American Dream," it was to be a private landholder. The Scotch-Irish shared that idealistic notion with all the other immigrant groups who came to America.

Religion was controlled in America (Puritans in Massachusetts, Anglicans in Virginia), but definitely not to the same extent as in the Old World. There was an excellent chance that the Scotch-Irish could avoid the strictures of the Test Act once they got to the New World. In fact, some members of Parliament had begun to grumble even in the 1690s about the laxity of controls exercised by the government over certain American colonies that were "too independently minded," and they singled out Pennsylvania in this regard. Perhaps that Parliamentary concern was one reason why so many Scotch-Irish ultimately made their way to William Penn's colony.

CHAPTER THREE

The Perils of the Deep

It is an understatement to say that by the early 1700s, America was the "promised land" to the Ulster Scots. It was a place, in their minds, of "limitless opportunity . . . where their skills . . . would be highly valued. America could not "fail to give freedom, peace, and plenty to those who now wish to enjoy those blessings."[1]

Attempts at Crossing

There had been attempts at Ulster immigration to the New World before the eighteenth century. The earlier settlers, some of whom went to the West Indies before proceeding to America, convinced many an Ulsterman back home to leave the religious and economic restrictions in north Ireland and come to the New World.

In 1636, just a few years after the Ulster Plantation was begun, two ministers in a small craft, *The Eagle Wing*, set out for America, but were turned back by stormy seas.[2] It was not until late in the century that further important migrations were made from Ulster.

Francis Makemie came to America in 1680, after settling first in Barbados for two years. He formed the Presbytery of Philadelphia, said to be the first presbytery in the New World.[3] Like most Scotch-Irish (clergy and lay alike), he was an itinerant wandering from Virginia to New York, preaching to whomever would hear him. Makemie frequently has been referred to as "The Father of American Presbyterianism."[4]

Even Makemie ran up against the long arm of the law when, on 20 January 1707, he preached in New York without first getting Governor Edward Hyde Cornbury's permission. Though ultimately acquitted of "preaching without a license," he still had to forfeit £83 of his hard earned money to the legal system to be rid of his troubles.[5]

In later times writer and poet Henry Van Dyke, was so entranced by Makemie's life that he penned this elegy to him.

> Oh who can tell how much we owe Thee
> Makemie, and to Labors such as thine.
> For all that makes America the shrine
> of faith untrammelled and of conscience free?
> Stand here, gray stone and consecrate the sod
> where sleeps this brave Scots-Irishman of God.[6]

Arrangements for Crossing

To be sure, most Scotch-Irish coming to America did not have as dramatic an impact as the good reverend Francis Makemie. In fact, a majority (especially in the latter half of the eighteenth century) came as indentured servants, willing to work four to seven years for a landowner in the American colonies in return for ship passage for themselves and families.[7]

An agent system of sorts was used; the agent served as an advance party, going to places in America and scouting the possibilities of settlement. The residents of the Bann Valley sent an agent to Boston in 1718,[8] an action that accounted in large part for New England being the first significant area of Scotch-Irish settlement in North America.[9]

Though the passengers left their native land with "some painful sensations,"[10] (they customarily made out their wills just before embarking)[11] and though they were risking a dangerous undertaking, the vast majority of crossings turned out safely. What was true for English voyages, as David Cressy has pointed out, also applied to the Scotch-Irish. The trips across the ocean on a crowded ship, he said, "could be likened to participants in a protracted *rite de passage*, enjoying an intensive form of *communitas*, while separated from their normal regime."[12] According to E. R. R. Green, the letters sent back home by young and unmarried immigrants described "a holiday. . . . Living conditions aboard the ships were cramped, but so were the farm houses at home. . . . The diet on the voyage was not unfamiliar as the immigrants brought their own food with them: oatmeal, potatoes, bacon, sugar, tea, and coffee."[13] Nevertheless, there were enough hazards to cause a would-be immigrant to think twice before taking himself (and often his family as well) over the Atlantic.[14]

Even at the beginning of the trip there was a considerable hazard, at least from the port of Belfast. On the way to the sea the channel "is so narrow and difficult that we must wait a favourable wind."[15] In the summertime, especially, an unpredictable southern wind prevailed, with the frequent result that ships were forced upon the shoals. Whenever these incidents occurred, the drinking water and most of the cargo had to be unloaded, causing delays of two to three weeks. Thus, many of the Scotch-Irish who finally did get off from Belfast left in a bad mood, which frequently got worse because of the conditions of the voyage.[16] Another hazard for the travelers was that most of the ships also carried goodly supplies of pitch, tar, turpentine, and logwood, constituting a real danger of fire.

The First Major Crossings

The first sizeable wave of Scotch-Irish immigration to America was in 1717–18, when some 5,000[17] Ulstermen decided to put themselves and their families at risk and spend anywhere from forty-two to ninety days crossing a wide, dangerous ocean. In July, 1728, seventeen ships were in North Irish ports, waiting to take passengers to North America. Over the course of the summer of 1728, some 3,000 persons left for New England and Pennsylvania.[18] A year later the number had increased: "Robert Gambie, a merchant in Londonderry . . . reported in July, 1729, 'There is gone and to go this Summer from this Port Twenty-five Sail of Ships, who carry each from One Hundred and forty passengers to America; there are many more going from Belfast; and the Ports near Colrain.' "[19]

Belfast was the principal port of embarkation, from whence New Castle, Delaware, and Philadelphia were the usual destinations; Larne, some thirty miles from Belfast, was the second largest, with many of its departing vessels bound for New York. In his book, *Ulster Immigration to Colonial America*, R. J. Dickson reported that a ship could legally transport one passenger for every twenty and a half square inches of deck space, a situation that made these Ulster craft worse than those used in the African slave trade. "When one passenger attempted to cross from one end of the vessel to another, the remaining portion were compelled to crowd themselves into one dense mass, many of them obliged to clamber on top of the chests."[20] Not until well into the nineteenth century did Parliament pass laws regulating the number of passengers that could be carried on an immigration vessel. From 1700 until 1850 the Scotch-Irish immigrant ships remained small, dirty, overcrowded, and dangerous.

Why People Left Ulster

A decade after the first general sailings, the English authorities stirred themselves to try to discover why so many Ulstermen were leaving. A commission was appointed, and on 26 June 1729, it sent its findings to the Privy Council. The Commission sympathized to some extent with those heading for the New World. Bad harvests in the late 1720s had produced multiple hardships, two of which were the precipitous rise in the price of corn and the disastrous drop in the price of linens. Rent raising had continued during these times of trouble, the Commission found, and clergy had pushed steadfastly, even bringing suit in some cases, to collect tithes from farmers who had seen their income dwindle on a daily basis.[21] The "multiplicity of the business of our circuit," however, kept the commissioners from learning whether these complaints were "well-grounded or exaggerated." These reasons notwithstanding, the commissioners felt—and here they made it clear that they were not so busy to discover right reason—that most people from North Ireland left for purely "selfish" reasons. They expected to find "great advantages" in New England and Pennsylvania and had been led to such conclusions by rosy, "unrealistic" letters from those who had gone before. Shipping companies and ship captains, however, gave the greatest incentives, the Commission charged, by painting idyllic pictures of the New World and frequently offering free passage to a head of household. These shipping companies, it was asserted, had become large landowners in America, and it was definitely in their best economic interests to get people to settle on them. (It must be noted, however, that shipping companies did not advertise heavily until the 1750s.) And, finally, in an ill-tempered, mean-spirited, and unjustified swipe against the Ulstermen's honesty, the Commission charged that "many dishonest and ill-designing people, to avoid payments of their just debts get on board ships . . . [whose captains] . . . conceal them from their creditors by refusing to let any persons see who is on board."[22]

Another report of 1729, by a "Gentleman in the North of Ireland," gave a conclusion opposite that of the Commission's: "It is indeed very amazing, that after all the risques and dangers that people have run, and the many misfortunes they have fallen under in those attempts, some having perished at sea, some robb'd by pirates, many of them cheated and abused by the villainy of masters of ships . . . [the immigrants are] still running in greater numbers than ever."[23] The "Gentleman" argued that the travelers were the "discreetist of people," and were not undertaking voyages merely from feelings of "giddiness and infatuation," because the "poor people are in great perplexity and trouble [in Ulster] . . . and know not what to do." His report predicted that "if a stop is not . . . put to this course . . . we shall have few Protestant dissenters left in this part of the Kingdom."[24]

Despite the work of the Privy Counsel Commission, no real steps were taken by the English government to stem the immigrations until just before the outbreak of the American Revolution, the reason generally being that as long as the French and their Indian allies fought England in the New World, England needed the Scotch-Irish.

Aboard The Ships

The only thing the immigrant ship offered was transportation, and a daily portion of drinking water. The passenger had to provide his own food, clothing, and bedding. This agreement with an immigrant, Hugh Scott, was typical: "The Bearer, Hugh Scott and his party, consisting of eight other persons is entitled to their passage in the Second Cabin of the Ship *Nightsdale*, bound for New York. They finding own provisions, bed and bedding. The ship finding berths, water, and fuel only."[25]

In some cases, people became stowaways, secretly getting aboard a ship and then avoiding the Captain and crew en route. One such stowaway was Hugh Todd, who escaped from Ireland by being rolled on board in a molasses barrel. According to the Todd family (of Pennsylvania) their temperaments have always been sweet because of the experiences of their forebear.[26]

The greatest difficulties these Scotch-Irish immigrants experienced on the way to America were storms at sea, squalls, pirates, calms, scarcities of water and food, and illnesses. One immigrant, William James Young, reported that on his boat, the *William*, one hundred of 119 passengers were seasick by the second day out of Belfast. On the sixth day at sea, a hurricane struck the *William*, causing great alarm and confusion:

> Chests, barrels, boxes, trunks, kettles, pots, pans, and in fact every moveable article were tossed about in all directions. This

> and the darkness that prevailed caused such a scene as may be conceived but cannot be described. Men, women, and children call for relief and pray most ernestly for God to send them help. . . . At this period I can safely say that there was not a single passenger on board but conceived they had only a few minutes to spend on this side of eternity.[27]

During the storm, a rumor started that the Captain and crew had abandoned ship and deserted their passengers by taking the long boat back to land. The rumor, said Young, caused a "most ludicrous scene to take place. A man . . . on hearing the report jumped out of bed, naked, left his wife behind, got up the ladder, and burst open the hatchway, got on deck and bawled out as loud as he could for the Captain to bring back the boat and take him along."[28]

As it turned out, Captain Lanmour was still aboard, along with his crew, and they rode out the storm. One odd thing, Young noted, was that all the storms they encountered raged for a day or two, then quit abruptly, and were immediately followed by periods of calm, during which the ship would make little or no progress. It was a matter, he asserted, of "having everything," or "having nothing;" there seemed to be no balance between the two extremes. The first evening after the storm abated, the passengers were so high spirited still to be alive that they held a deck party in celebration. Johnny the cook, and Young himself, danced Irish jigs for the pleasure of the other passengers until the late hour of ten. Next morning, though, came the job of "regulating affairs" and "cleaning out" after the storm: "After so much sickness, I dare not try to give a description of any part of the vessel."[29]

John Craig (later of great Presbyterian fame in America) made the crossing from 10 June to 17 August in 1734. On the way over, he was "sore afflicted with seasickness which brought me very low." The most remarkable thing that happened to Craig was that he was apparently washed off the ship, but lived to tell about it: "I Escaped a very Imminent danger of being lost in a manner almost miraculous without any mean but ye kind hand of Providence being accidentally cast overboard in a Dark and tempestuous Night. Lay as on a bed of Down on my back on the Raging Wave which tos'd back on ye Ship's Side where I found holds, and Sprung Aboard."[30] Craig took his miraculous rescue as "Evidence of Divine Care [which] I ought Ever to Remember with a Gratefull & Thankfull heart to His Praise & Glory who made the proud wave a bed but not a Grave to Swallow me up without Remidy."[31]

Though not thrown overboard, another Scotch-Irish diarist, Jonathan Moore, nevertheless believed that storms at sea should humble a person and cause him to seek divine help for his salvation. He and his sister boarded the *Snow Cape Breton* in 1760 at Larne, bound for New York. While most of the immigrants were devout, Moore reported, the same could not be said of the ship's crew:

> It is really a matter of astonishment to me that sailors who go down to the sea in ships and do business in great waters can see the works of the Lord and His wonders in the great deep should, in general, with respect to Christianity, be such abandoned, stupid mortals. All their discourse is filled with oaths and obscenities. The more dreadful the storm, the more horrid their oaths and blasphemy, and they seem to study by all possible means to stifle all serious, rational thought. They do not just curse God, or I should compare them to nothing but infernal imps."[32]

Many accounts of voyages across spoke of squalls or gales that lasted five or six hours, and then quit just as suddenly as they had appeared. Young wrote of a "tremendous squall" that hit his ship, the *William*. A sudden change of wind laid the ship nearly on her side, "and before she righted was struck several times by heavy seas and waves rising half mast. . . . It was found necessary to strip the vessel of all her sails and just when completed, it pleased Providence to check the storm, and in ten minutes from it being at its height we had the pleasure of finding the wind to cease and the sea to give up its roaring and in a few minutes were nearly becalmed."[33]

Many times these ships encountered contrary winds and

were blown off course, and frequently—particularly if the vessel were headed for New York or Boston—would find themselves in the vicinity of icebergs. Diarist Moore saw "several islands of ice" as he rode the *Snow Cape Breton* to America. Some of these icebergs, he said, at first looked like other ships, but then up close they "appeared in a hundred different shapes."[34] A letter writer from Boston explained that his voyage had been tedious and hard. "I can say we had not Thirty Hours fair wind the whole time." There were "large stands of ice on the banks of Newfoundland, . . . running foul of one in foggy weather." Running leeward of the berg, the ship was becalmed and only with "great difficulty" did the captain get his ship and passengers out of the dangerous situation.[35]

When the Scotts came over, their ship, the *Nightsdale*, nearly ran into an iceberg. The terrified passengers were made to go down into the hold, and the hatches were battened down. They could hear scraping sounds, and thought they were doomed.[36] What they heard were the long pointed poles—standard equipment for just about any ship of that day—being used by the sailors to keep the ship away from the iceberg. The *Nightsdale*, after six weeks at sea, finally made it to New York.

Danger From Pirates

In addition to the natural calamities that threatened the immigrants, there were some man-made ones as well. Piracy was rife throughout the eighteenth and much of the nineteenth centuries, and sea passengers were constantly in jeopardy of life and limb. Young, aboard the *William*, gave a graphic description of a close encounter with what was surely a pirate ship:

> Perceived a sail at a distance ahead. In the course of the day made nearer. In the evening she stood for us. [that is, she came within boarding distance]. . . . Many of our passengers had

retired to rest. In a few minutes the alarm was given and all but two hurried to get on deck. . . . The Captain spoke to the stranger, but was answered in a foreign language unintelligible. This confirmed the general opinion that the stranger must be a pirate and that we were about to be boarded by her crew, to be robbed of everything we were possessed of, and perhaps to be murdered. No other thing now appeared evident but that an engagement must take place, and all men flew to arms. Some of the most heroic soon appeared armed with knives, forks, hammers, brush handles, and many other war like weapons. . . . Eleven O'clock came and still the same suspense prevailed, the ships lying so close to each other that there was the great danger of their rigging getting entangled. . . . It was now conceived by some that the strangers intended waiting for day light before they would board us. One O'clock and . . . nearly all the women had got on deck. To endeavor to save property and provisions from the enemy was now the lookout of many. Some were hiding their money. . . . Others were putting on as many as could of their best clothes."

At two o'clock the "dreaded antagonist," for some reason, made sail, "which prevented our men from displaying that bravery and heroism so common to the crew and passengers of an Irish ship." Different opinions prevailed, but it was "generally supported that finding ours to be a passenger vessel, and seeing so many brave fellows on deck they did not think it worth risking an attack."[37]

The Deadly Calms

Added to the problems of storms, squalls, icebergs, and pirates, was another one which, all told, was probably the deadliest. This was the calm, brought on by prevailing easterly winds which slowed the ship's progress toward the west or, more often than not, no wind at all. In these situations the ship simply sat for days or weeks at a time. In a good passage, six weeks got a passenger from Belfast to Philadelphia, but if the ship were becalmed, twice that long and more was not unusual.

Drinking water was the most precious commodity in these calms, and sometimes its supply was entirely spent with several days still remaining at sea. Food was the next essential to be depleted. Some survivors of these ordeals later described their experiences either through diaries or letters to the *Belfast Newsletter*, a newspaper that became a conduit by which settlers in America got messages to their loved ones still in Ireland. The *Newsletter* also helped to make the government aware of the squalid condition of the immigrant vessels and urged that companies themselves be held accountable if not enough provisions were taken along.

Young described the effects of a calm on their water supply: "Since coming on board our allowance of water each day was two quarts for adults and one for children. . . . But this day [during the calm] water (I have to call it so here but were I at home I would call it a poisonous liquid) . . . was found to be so far run [out], and an order was issued and carried into effect to stop a pint off each person's allowance. This being done, we are in great want in the evening. Not a drop to quench our thirst, and the heat [is] insufferable."[38]

A few days later, though, the passengers delighted in seeing a rain storm ahead of them. Young said that it "came on a smart shower," and while it rained, he turned his umbrella wrong side up, and gleefully collected six quarts of precious water, "which proved the greatest treat we had since leaving Ireland. I now found that water was one of the most valuable gifts that the Almighty has bestowed upon us."[39]

Passengers on many other ships were not as fortunate as Young and his compatriots aboard the *William*. In 1729, according to R. J. Dickson, 175 people died on two crossings of the Atlantic. Six of forty-six passengers aboard the *Seaflower* died, and were apparently consumed by the survivors.[40] Three hundred immigrants set out on the *General Wolfe* in 1772; eighty of them died, and those who ultimately landed were "mere skeletons so weak they could hardly walk or stand."[41]

The *Sallie*, sailing from Larne to Philadelphia in 1762, was truly an ill-fated ship. Advertised in the *Belfast Newsletter* as a "fine new ship . . . one of the fastest sailing vessels . . .

properly provided with proper accommodations for passengers,"[42] it was immediately detained on suspicion of having wool aboard, in violation of the Woolens Act, which forbade Ulster wool to go anywhere except to England and Wales. Having resolved that problem, the 300 ton *Sallie* finally weighed anchor on 15 April 1762, commanded by James Taylor. But bad luck beset the ship and was documented by passenger Robert Smilie, who kept a journal of the voyage, that his father in Ireland published in the *Belfast Newsletter*, causing a considerable sensation among those who read it.

When the *Sallie* left Larne, it had a full allowance of bread and water for just two weeks. (A constant complaint of passengers was that captains were grossly negligent in estimating the amount of provisions for the trip across, resulting in a near depletion of supplies when they reached the New World on even the best of voyages. If contrary winds held back the ship, or if it came into a calm, provisions, scanty to begin with, became critical).

Southwest winds drove the *Sallie* north into a wet, frigid climate. One day a squall of wind lasted three hours, and a few days later, a gale beset them for nine hours. After the storms, they had to fight off icebergs, and they drifted south because "our weather became extremely warm." In August 1762, the *Sallie* hit a calm that Smilie and the other passengers feared would be fatal. After the tenth day of the calm, bread rations were reduced to two and a half pounds per week for each passenger. Then the weekly portion was limited to one and a half pounds, and for twelve days each passenger had only two biscuits for the entire time. They did have a half noggin of barley each day, which they ate raw, for they did not have any water suitable for boiling; in fact, they were daily limited to a half pint of water for each passenger.[43]

Smilie gave a vivid picture of what it was like to suffer through an extended calm: "Hunger and thirst had now reduced our crew to the last extremity; nothing was now to be heard aboard our ship but the cries of distressed children, and of their distressed mothers, unable to relieve them. Our ship now was truly a real spectacle of Horror! Never a Day passed without one or two of our crew put overboard; Many killed themselves by drinking salt water; and their own Urine was a Common Drink; yet in the midst of all our miseries, Our Captain showed not the least remorse or pity."[44]

At long last, on 2 September 1762, John Smilie spotted land, and knew that they were approaching Philadelphia. Since the *Sallie* had left Larne in the spring, that meant it had been at sea between fourteen and fifteen weeks. On the voyage sixty-four passengers died and were buried at sea.[45]

Problems of Contagious Diseases

Very frequently after these long, painful voyages, the all but exhausted travelers had to endure yet another three to seven weeks in quarantine if various contagious diseases were rampaging. Word was received in all the American ports that cholera was a persistent problem in Belfast, and many ships arriving from Ireland were quarantined for sixteen days. Despite Young's ordeals aboard the *William*, the visiting doctor at the Port of Baltimore declared the ship to be "the cleanest that had arrived during the season, and the passengers to be in the best order."[46]

"Ship fever," covered a variety of contagious ailments on the way across, and claimed many lives.[47] No malady, however, struck fear into the hearts of people as much as smallpox. One immigrant, Alexander Chesney, remarked that "there is no disorder the Americans are so much afraid of as the smallpox, and with good reason."[48] His little sister, Peggy, died of the illness on the way from Larne to Charlestown (Charleston), South Carolina. "The smallpox was very severe in the vessel during the passage." The surgeon at Charleston forced Chesney and all the other passengers to stay aboard the ship for another seven weeks,[49] which approximated the length of the voyage itself.

Some ship captains, though, who became known to the authorities through the years, could sometimes use their influence to get smallpox exposed passengers ashore. One passenger reported: "Smallpox broke out in the vessel and occasioned the deaths of some children. Our worthy captain and the Reverend . . . were duly employed visiting the sick and administering cordials. The smallpox would have put a quarantine of six weeks upon us had not the Captain [intervened] by an application to a friend of his through whose kind mediation we obtained liberty to go ashore."[50]

Many health officials at major American ports had long complained that premature debarkations of immigrants had contributed significantly to smallpox epidemics. The charge was not entirely unjustified.

Sometimes, even if a ship were disease free, it came upon a port where epidemics of yellow fever, cholera, or smallpox raged. In such cases, the unfortunate passengers were detained aboard the vessel for days and weeks, waiting for the medical authorities to release them.

The men, women, and children who sailed on these immigrant ships were hardy folk to begin with, and though they may have been physically weakened by crossing the Atlantic, the experience only hardened them in their ways of endurance, independence, and willfulness. Richard Hofstadter, quoting the agriculturalist, Arthur Young, noted: "Men who immigrate are, from the nature of circumstances, the most active, hardy, daring, bold and resolute spirits, and probably the most mischievous also."[51]

It was not until 1773, as troubles grew between the American colonies and the Mother Country that Parliament tried to curb Scotch-Irish immigration, but by that time a quarter million Scotch-Irish immigrants had arrived in American ports. Before this year, while France had been England's greatest enemy in America, England had actually encouraged the Scotch-Irish to immigrate. They made excellent fighters against the French and, after some painful indoctrinations, against the American Indians. They were good people to have around in a time of crisis.

CHAPTER FOUR

Settling In The New World

It was not solely the American experience that hardened the Scotch-Irish pioneers. Their ordeals in Ulster had helped them to become durable long before they reached the shores of North America. If they survived the perilous crossings of the Atlantic, they took such to mean that God had saved them for a purpose, and they felt obligated to him for their lives and well-being. Once they got to North America, the Scotch-Irish adapted to New World necessities: "The history of the Ulsterman in America . . . is less a matter of the working out of hereditary characteristics on the frontier . . . than a series of adjustments to changing circumstances."[1]

New England Settlements

Many Scotch-Irish agents picked New England as the most likely place for these unsettled people to live. After all, the Puritans of Massachusetts, like the Scotch-Irish themselves, were Calvinists; thus, the Scotch-Irish believed they would be welcomed by their Puritan brethren.

The first Scotch-Irish settlers in New England came in 1718, when, in July and August of that year, five ships arrived at

Boston harbor from Derry, Coleraine, and Belfast, carrying 120 families.[2] Over the next several years, some 20,000 Ulstermen came to New England.[3]

The Puritans in Boston did not take to the Scotch-Irish, even though some Bostonians saw the value of Scotch-Irish assistance against the Indians.[4] Though they were both of the Calvinist persuasion, it was, as historian Maury Klein put it, a "confrontation between marble and granite."[5] The Puritans and Scotch-Irish were alike in their religious rigidity and their unwillingness to have anything to do with other creeds. The Puritans expected the Scotch-Irish to support the established church of Puritanism if they wanted to stay in Massachusetts.[6]

So many were coming, too, that the Puritans feared that the Scotch-Irish would "eat us up."[7] Old Cotton Mather fumed that the Scotch-Irish represented "the formidable attempts of Satan and his Sons to unsettle us."[8] Many of the Scotch-Irish arrived in Boston indigent and had to be cared for to some extent by agencies of the General Court, an action that only furthered the resentment against the Scotch-Irish, whom the Bostonians referred to simply as "Irish."[9] There was some snobbery involved. In the eyes of many Bostonians, the newcomers were slovenly in appearance (who would not be after six to eight weeks on an ocean?), rough of speech, illiterate, and—some at least—hard drinkers.[10] In other words, they were not "cultured"; and thus were unacceptable to the prim Bostonians.

A final reason why the Scotch-Irish were unwelcome in Massachusetts was that there apparently was not enough good farm land to go around. Accordingly, there was not as much need for the indentured labor system in New England as in other parts of the country.[11]

The Scotch-Irish began to spread out from the Boston area, and their first major outpost was Worcester. The same procedure applied at Worcester as at Boston. At first, the Scotch-Irish were welcome because they could be useful in the event of Indian attacks. Then, the Scotch-Irish grew increasingly unhappy with having to support the Puritan ministry, and petitioned the town authorities for an exemption.[12] The petition failing, many Scotch-Irish in 1736 began building their own church, where their own religious creeds could be practiced. "When the structure was well begun, the Puritan inhabitants of Worcester [and Pelham] gathered in the dark of night, leveled the structure to the ground, and burned or carried off the building materials."[13]

Spreading Into Other Areas

From Massachusetts, the Scotch-Irish went to the territory of Maine, where the potato plants that they had brought with them from Ireland thrived.[14] They are also credited with introducing the spinning wheel and the manufacture of linen products to the British American colonies.[15]

Remembering their experiences in Massachusetts, some Scotch-Irish, notably David Dunbar, began a separatist movement in Maine, trying to become a colony independent of the Puritans. The Massachusetts magistrates would have none of this and in 1732 persuaded Parliament to disavow Dunbar, who had returned to England. He was imprisoned for debt and then released and appointed as Governor of St. Helena in the South Atlantic.

Before the Bay Colony reasserted its powers, however, Maine territory became a place of intense Scotch-Irish settlement. One hundred fifty Presbyterian families moved into the territory, beginning such towns as Harrington, Walpole, and Townsend.[16] Samuel Waldo was responsible for additional Scotch-Irish settlement in Maine. In 1735, he gave twenty-seven families one hundred acres each along the St. George River.[17] Later in the century, the towns of Stirling and Belfast were established in Maine territory, both peopled by settlers from Ulster.

Another place to which the Scotch-Irish fled out of Massachusetts was New Hampshire. Even as early as 1718, when the first large waves of immigrants were arriving in New England, some sixteen families moved to Nutfield, New Hampshire, renaming it Londonderry. Over the next several years refugees from Massachusetts poured into the New Hampshire colony, founding such localities as Windham, Derryfield, and Chester. The descendants of these earliest New Hampshire settlers also moved into various places in Vermont and Rhode Island. Thus, by 1750 there was a strong Scotch-Irish presence in New England. Author George F. Smyth estimated in 1883 that fully 100,000 persons had descended from the early settlers of Londonderry, New Hampshire. "There is, probably, not a State in the Union today [1883] without some of the descendants of this colony, first planted in the wilderness by sixteen families in 1718."[18]

The Puritans of Massachusetts were like the Anglicans in Ireland: they drove the Scotch-Irish out from among them. Maine, New Hampshire, Vermont, and Rhode Island, became places of religious refuge, not from wild-eyed Anglican radicals in England and Ireland, but from rigidly fixed Puritans in Massachusetts.

Pennsylvania Becomes Attractive

Once the Scotch-Irish in Ulster got wind of Boston's unfriendliness, they began to concentrate on other destinations, notably Philadelphia. William Penn's colony was exceptional among the British North American possessions. Its authorities generally got along with the Indians, taxes were among the lowest in the American colonies, good land was available, and "military service unheard of because of the Quaker commitment to pacifism."[19] On the whole, Pennsylvania was a place where people of many different religious persuasions had lived together in harmony. The immigrants arriving in Philadelphia in the 1720s were mostly German and Scotch-Irish. Those who had not been able to pay for their passages "bound themselves out to ship companies, who auctioned them off to the highest bidders . . . or sold them as a lot to a merchant dealing in human merchandise."[20] The Germans, of Lutheran beliefs, practically co-settled Pennsylvania and other parts of the country with the Scotch-Irish.

Along with its religious liberalism, Pennsylvania had an indenture system that was attractive to most newcomers. In return for four or five years work, the colonizer would be given a fifty acre tract of land upon which to provide a living for himself and family. These were reckoned to be good terms, particularly by comparison with what the Scotch-Irish had left behind in Ulster. Of most importance, those fifty acres granted to a man after his indenture were his. He owned them; there was no rent, either short-term or long-term, to be paid on these acres. In addition, he could add to his holdings in accordance with his financial capabilities. Over and over this message of owning land, self sufficiency, and being one's own master was sent back to the Old Country by immigrants, creating new impulses for traveling west.

In 1700 the population of Pennsylvania was some 20,000; in 1750, it was 250,000.[21] Most of these new Pennsylvanians were German, but a large minority was Scotch-Irish. The southern part of Lancaster County in Pennsylvania attracted the immigrants from Ulster; so much so that one person said that in Lancaster County, "there were more Scotch-Irish than people."[22] Robert Galt is said to have been the first Presbyterian settler in Lancaster County, crossing the Octorara Hills in 1709 and settling in the Pequea Valley.[23]

James Logan was Pennsylvania's provincial secretary and himself an immigrant from Largan, in Ulster. He was keen to participate in William Penn's "glorious experiment" of creating a polyglot society, where people of all faiths and nationalities could come and live peacefully among one another. Thus he let it be known that the Scotch-Irish would be welcome. He knew them to be stubborn and prideful but at the same time, strong and resourceful, just the kind of people who could be of optimum assistance in building a new society.

But Logan was not quite prepared for the consequences of his invitation. In the early part of the eighteenth century, the province of Ulster had a population of some half a million, out of which about 250,000 were Presbyterian.[24] Between the 1720s and 1768, approximately one-third of the Protestant population of Ireland immigrated to British North America, and overwhelmingly they came to Pennsylvania.[25]

Scotch-Irish Activities in Pennsylvania

The first major problem with the Scotch-Irish in Pennsylvania was their tendency to appropriate lands unto themselves—no matter that very frequently these lands had already been granted to someone else. As historian Maury Klein explained: "Lacking funds to purchase land, the Scotch-Irish simply settled where they pleased. . . . They came in such great numbers that neither proprietors nor officials could keep up with their movements. Every attempt to collect purchase price or expel them from the land was strenuously resisted."[26]

Logan estimated in 1726 that Scotch-Irish squatters occupied 100,000 acres of Pennsylvania land. They justified their actions by invoking the Deity, saying that it was "against the laws of God and Nature, that so much land should be idle while so many Christians wanted it to labor on, and to raise their bread."[27]

Their practice of squatting earned the Scotch-Irish a bad reputation in some parts. They had been so land-starved in the Old World, however, and had been so victimized by absentee landlordism that they were at ease in simply taking land and growing food on it. It was probably their taking of land that caused an unjustified stereotype of the Irish and the Scotch-Irish to begin: "The Scotch-Irish keep the Sabbath and just about everything else they come across too."

In addition to squatting on lands already granted to English and German colonists, the Scotch-Irish thought nothing of dispossessing Indian tribes of their property. The Ulster Scots had already removed one people, the native Irish, to make room for themselves, and in the same way they did not regard the Indians as the rightful owners of these lands but as obstacles in the way of Christian progress.

The Scotch-Irish actions against the Indians—which often bordered on ruthlessness—were in direct contrast with all previous Quaker policies. The Quakers had always acquired lands from the Indians through treaty and by paying for the possessions they took. One of the best known and most admired qualities of William Penn, the founding proprietor of Pennsylvania, was that he treated Indians as his friends and equals.[28] Now the Scotch-Irish began to put all those good Pennsylvania-Indian relationships into jeopardy. Their actions would have serious consequences in the years ahead, particularly in the 1750s, when a series of dreadful Indian wars broke out between the Pennsylvania colonists and the Indians.

Almost as soon as they got to southern Lancaster County, the Scotch-Irish became politically active, challenging the dominance of the Quaker party. The Scotch-Irish thought the Quakers too lenient toward the Indians and not aggressive enough in selling and cultivating the land.

An early example of Scotch-Irish politicking may be seen in the case of Andrew Galbraith. In 1729, he stood for election to the provincial assembly for Donegal Township against George Stewart, a Quaker. The two conducted spirited campaigns and Galbraith emerged as the victor. His wife Ann was credited with his victory. Though women in Ulster had not been greatly political, they seem to have become so once they reached the New World. Ann Galbraith campaigned over much of Lancaster County, where Donegal Township was located, going from one place to another on the back of her favorite mare, and giving eloquent speeches to many audiences on behalf of her husband. Andrew Galbraith's election ended Quaker political domination of the township.[29] In all the places in Pennsylvania where the Scotch-Irish settled (primarily in Lancaster County), the same effort undertaken by Andrew Galbraith occurred; that is, challenging Quaker authority and defeating it in one election after another.

Andrew's brother, John, was elected sheriff of Lancaster County in 1731. John Bayley, another Scotch-Irish immigrant, became justice of the peace; Alexander Lowry served in the colonial general assembly, and for a time was even the commissioner for Indian Affairs, an incongruous position indeed for a Scotch-Irishman. Other early settlers in Lancaster

County to distinguish themselves politically included Patrick Campbell, John Sterret, and James Keys, who served as sheriffs, assemblymen, and colonial senators.[30] In the years to come, Scotch-Irish influence over Pennsylvania politics became significant, fulfilling Logan's prediction of 1725: "If the Scotch-Irish continue to come they will make themselves proprietors of the province [of Pennsylvania]."[31]

Scotch-Irish and "American"

To those early Scotch-Irish in Pennsylvania must go some of the credit for establishing what later became known as "American" culture and national character. Pennsylvania was the "cultural nursery" of North America[32] where the basic foundations were laid for the spread of American civilization. As one author put it, "the single homestead and unincorporated hamlet and a system of land use dominated by corn and livestock economy"[33] were the patterns set in Pennsylvania by the Scotch-Irish, patterns that subsequently dominated the settlement of much of the continent.

When the Scotch-Irish came into a community, there were four stages of settling in. First, they constructed crude forts to protect themselves from Indian attacks; second, they built a church; third, if they could provide the necessary teacher for it, they added a school; and fourth, they erected permanent houses for themselves.[34]

The Importance of Churches

It was the church that gained most of the Scotch-Irishman's attention. After all, he felt that he had paid a dear price for the right to his own church service without having to conform to someone else's version of Christianity. It was for this reason that places of worship were built before permanent residences.

In the places where the Scotch-Irish settled, churches were built approximately eleven miles from each other, for this distance could accommodate the capacities of horses pulling buggies to church. No-one would have to drive more than five or six miles to get to the meeting.

Also, most of the early Presbyterian churches, particularly in Pennsylvania, were located at large springs as a matter of preference. If such were not available, creeks or small rivers would do. The reason for the location was that Sunday services lasted all day, and sometimes the extended meetings went on for a week at a time, necessitating the essentials of water and food.

The identity of the oldest Presbyterian church founded by the Scotch-Irish in America is still rather hotly debated. Since the Scotch-Irish came into the Delaware River after they had made the Atlantic crossing, many historians have made the logical claim that the very first Scotch-Irish settlements were around what is today New Castle, Delaware. According to one author, however, the oldest church in the United States of Scotch-Irish descent is Rebohah, or "Makemie's Church," in Maryland.[35]

Some Pennsylvania Churches

While they might not be the oldest, there are still some aged and famous Scotch-Irish Presbyterian churches in Pennsylvania. Two of the most notable are Donegal (spelled "Dunagull" until the mid eighteenth century) and Middle Spring. These two churches typified all the others that the Scotch-Irish established.

The Donegal Church dates from 1720. It was a ten-by-sixteen-foot log structure, as were most other Presbyterian churches of that time. (Later, the church builders utilized field stone, making a practice of using no stone that could not be lifted by just one man, a symbol of individual strength being lifted "unto the Lord.") At one end of the little structure were steps leading up to a small balcony where, on pretty sabbaths, the minister would preach to the congregation as they sat "among the graves and under the trees."[36] After the preaching, the congregants sang hymns, following the lead of a "precentor" who "lined out" the words and tunes. The reason for "lining out" was not that the worshippers were illiterate, but that there were not enough hymn books to go around.[37]

Donegal Church was built near a spring which, one estimate put it, emitted two million gallons of water a day.[38] At Donegal a favorite legend grew through the years about a horse. The story went that when the original frame structure was demolished and replaced by a stone building, an old horse was used to haul the stones to the construction site. Just as the walls of the new building were in place, the horse died, and its head was buried under the pulpit, keeping up an old Irish tradition of "burying esteemed animals under the hearth."[39] (In 1958, workmen putting heating ducts into the church found the skeletal remains of a horse's head buried under the pulpit so many years before. The horse legend is still very popular fare at Donegal Presbyterian Church.)

The Middle Spring Presbyterian Church dates from the early 1730s and is located near Shippensburg, Pennsylvania. One of its earliest pastors was a Reverend Cooper, who called the roll every Sunday morning to see who of his congregation was missing. During the subsequent week, he would visit each absentee and demand that he give a reason for being away from church. Also, he required that his members sing a psalm to completion before leaving for services each Sunday morning.

David Herron was one of the steadiest, most faithful members of the Middle Spring Church. One Sunday, though, he shocked the whole congregation by being absent. Sure enough, the next day the Reverend Cooper went after him. Herron gave this explanation: "Yesterday morning I got up a little earlier than usual; ate a little breakfast; read a short chapter; then we kneeled, and said a short prayer, and I commenced, with the family, to sing a Psalm, the one in course being the 119th [the longest Psalm in the Old Testament]. I could not violate your rules; I could not pass over it; I did my best, but was not able to finish it until in the afternoon."[40] Mollified, the Reverend accepted the explanation and excused Herron's absence.

Power and Influence of Presbyterian Churches

Examples such as Herron's absence showed the great power that pastors and elders of Presbyterian churches wielded over their charges. One minister wrote back to Scotland about a certain member of his congregation who was censured for "washing himself on the Lord's Day."[41] But an action like this was quite mild compared to some of the remonstrances and outright punishment meted out to infractious members of Presbyterian churches. Sometimes, special committees were created to act as a sort of a grand jury, to investigate alleged misdeeds of church members. Frequently, with the evidence facing them, the offenders were required to stand before the entire congregation and confess their sins. Failure to do so meant expulsion from the church and ostracism from the community.

In 1742, three Presbyterian Churches in Pennsylvania began a cooperative "sessions" book. Middle Spring, Big Springs, and Rocky Springs, kept a comprehensive record of its investigations, findings, and sentences. In many instances, these combined church activities took the place of civil and even criminal courts in the area. Most of the offenses these churches dealt with would today undoubtedly go before some government court. It is also questionable whether any church today, Scotch-Irish Presbyterian or otherwise, would delve as deeply into its members' private lives as their counterparts of two centuries ago. Subjects that these church courts dealt with quite frequently were marriage problems, public scandals, differences of opinion with Presbyterian doctrine, slander, quarrels, "immodesty" (that is, illicit love affairs between men and women), perjury, boundary and property disputes, false witnessing, domestic altercations, protection of women against lascivious men, and "loose language."

The sessions among the three churches ruled that no marriage could be officiated without prior application of the parties to the minister and his approval. Also, in any dispute between or among persons, every opportunity would be taken to get the parties themselves to conciliate their problems. Only when this procedure failed would the sessions become involved. If a person disagreed with the judgment of the sessions, he could appeal it to the nearest presbytery. This process of appeal, in fact, gave the Presbyterian Church a somewhat representational feature before such procedures were established by any civil government in North America.

No matter was too trivial for the sessions to look into: "A. P. entered a complaint against D. S. for hurting her character by reporting that she had a Hankerchiefe of his which he lost at the Middle Spring Meeting House." After listening to a parade of witnesses, the sessions decided that D. S. had slandered A. P., noting that A. P.'s handkerchief was merely similar in appearance to D. S.'s, and that he had acted sinfully in accusing her.

There was a report "that there has been something immodest between J. M. and M. L." The sessions learned that though "the Devil was busy driving Temptations into M. L.'s head," she and J. M. were largely the victims of innuendoes and community gossip. One rebellious party involved let it be known that "If the sessions didn't look to themselves about the Affair, he wou'd look to them." This person was cited to appear before the church group to explain his language, but the records do not indicate whether or not he obeyed.

A. M. objected to R. M.'s becoming a deacon because R. M. had "sundry times" abused A. M. "with his tongue, as also his wife, when he wasn't present." Going further into the matter of A. M. and R. M., the sessions found that a boundary dispute generated the heat between them. Two members of the session were appointed to adjudicate the landowners' problems. Both men were found to be "ungodly" in their treatment of each other. R. M. "acted very wrong in twitting A. M." and A. M. "us'd some very unbecoming and sinfull expressions, unsuitable to a Christian profession." The sessions ordered that R. M. and A. M. "be admonished . . . and require that hereupon they be reconcil'd & be at peace." Both parties agreed to the judgement, ended their disputes, and became good friends.

Further showing its power and influence, the sessions disciplined R. M. for saying to A. M. "that if he shou'd live beside A. M. 20 or 40 years . . . he wou'd still have a grudge & ill will at him, & cou'd not help it." Under prodding from the sessions, R. M. admitted the intemperance of his language, and repented of it. Still other affairs dealt with hearing about a young woman who had to fend off an ardent suitor with a churn dash; not accepting the testimony of people still in their minority; forcing a member of the congregation who was chronically absent from church to stand up and say why; admonishing J. P. for taking venison from an Indian; and others for numerous breaches of the sabbath, such as working, trading, or fishing.[42]

None of these activities, however, came even close to the misuse of liquor and its consequences in keeping the sessions busy. The Scotch-Irish, despite their fundamentalism, were definitely not teetotalers. On the contrary, they earned a widespread reputation of being hard drinkers. At weddings, and even funerals, the Scotch-Irish brought their bottles with them. One minister, Alexander Craighead, owned an "elegant punch bowl and glasses, and what was served would hardly qualify today as 'Presbyterian punch.' "[43] Two preachers, the Reverends MacMillan and Patterson, offered joint services one night. Patterson prayed so long that MacMillan drank both glasses of whiskey that had been set before them. MacMillan answered Patterson's reproach by asserting that "on the frontier, you must watch as well as pray."[44]

While the Presbyterian ministers earned a widespread reputation of "being able to hold their liquor," such was not always so with the regular members of the various congregations. The Middle Spring sessions spent an inordinate amount of its time investigating and then pronouncing judgement, upon those brethren who had become too familiar with the bottle.

H. B., for example, appeared before the sessions and "acknowledged his sin in being out of order with liquor & profess'd that it had been a matter of sorrow and humiliation to him before the Lord & that he resolved thro' grace to watch against it for the future upon which the session think it proper that the moderator give him a caution about it."[45] At this same meeting, the sessions learned that W. C. "was the worse for liquor at S. C.'s Wedding as appear'd in that he was not cappable to govern himself as usual & that sitting on a bench at the end of the house, he fell back over." W. C. was cited by the sessions and admitted that he had been "too merry, jocose & loose in his conduct, and that he had drank more than he shou'd have done." The session rebuked W. C. "for his loose & intemperate conduct & behaviour unbecoming one professing Christianity."[46]

In another case, S. L. was so "disordered with liquor" that he was "not fully capable to sit straight on his Horse; & when stopped to get some Drink, he lighted, & cou'd'nt stand but reel'd to the other side opposite to the place where he was." M. E. had brought S. L. a "bason" full of beer, and as he drank it, "he sally'd as he stood" and "spill'd some of it."

S. L. talked his way out of most of his troubles with the sessions. He staggered after lighting from his horse, he claimed, because "the creature shoulder'd against him." Also, the "beer bason" was full, "& so possibly he might spill." The sessions ruled that S. L. had largely kept control of his faculties and that "his bad state of Health might contribute much to the disorder that appear'd in him, which gave Room to people to judge him guilty of intemperance." The sessions also decided, however, that liquor was the occasion "of stirring up his bodily disorders"; thus, he was admonished to be "more cautious in use of spiritous Liquors,"[47] a decision which S. L. readily accepted.

An almost unforgivable sin was for someone secretly to mix drinks at social occasions. Beer mixed with distilled liquor caused mayhem at J. L.'s wedding. Bad tempers, quarrels, and even a few fights occurred, all attributed to the "mixed liquors." The perpetrators ultimately confessed and were "severely censur'd" by the sessions.[48]

One of the inevitable consequences of intemperance was fist-fights, brawls, and even "riots," and the Middle Spring sessions dealt with them as they occurred. W. J. and A. H. got into a fracas at Shippensberg, and A. H. "abused W. J. on the face." He "catch'd him by the Hair & struck him on the face several stroaks, by which he made him bleed. . . ."[49] The two fighters were cited by the session and made to express great remorse for their sinful activities.

Trade fairs were quite popular with the Scotch-Irish where they demonstrated and sold foodstuffs and manufactured articles. But these fairs attracted an element that was excessively "raised by liquor." At one fair a man "spoke saucily" to T. E. who "struck him about the head." This altercation brought G. C., W. J., and J. C. into the matter, and a drunken brawl ensued. The Middle Spring session later rebuked all the parties to the incident and condemned their intemperance.

The difference between a "brawl" and a "riot" apparently was that a brawl was a spontaneous event while a riot was a planned, deliberate fight at fairs and other public places among rival groups. The men consumed prodigious quantities of alcohol before these events; thus, "bad blood" between groups, bolstered by strong spirits, sometimes produced dreadful results.

One such affair occurred in late 1743, when J. T., J. G., T. G., J. M., W. D., G. H., J. R., H. B., and several others involved themselves in a general "free for all." The Middle Spring session expressed its "great Abhorrence of the Piece of Conduct before them, as a tumultuous Riot thro' Intemperance in Drink, whereby the Laws of God are grossly violated, and Religion is expos'd to Reproach."[50] Those rioters subject to the jurisdiction of the session were severely rebuked and threatened with expulsion from the Presbyterian Church. They duly repented, and were restored to grace.

These examples show clearly that the Scotch-Irish experiences in the British North American colonies cannot be separated from religious activities. The Scotch-Irish may have been long suffering from their ordeals in the Old World, they may have been rigid in their ways and beliefs, but above everything else, they were human, subject to all the strengths and weaknesses of humanity in general.

The average Scotch-Irish miscreant greatly preferred going before a governmental rather than an ecclesiastical court. In the former, his punishment would be fines and perhaps confinement. In the latter, he had to bare his soul to the people he knew and loved best. Confessing his sins to his congregation and publicly repenting of them was one of the most humbling experiences a person could ever expect.

These examples show, too, that one must not look to the Scotch-Irish for any development of religious toleration in America. They were as set in their ways as the Puritans, firmly believing that God had chosen them to be his chief spokesmen on earth. Religious toleration in America got its first great impulse from Roger Williams in Rhode Island, and from there evolved in the rest of the country throughout the next two hundred years. Historian Richard Hofstadter makes a distinction between religious *freedom*, which the Scotch-Irish were apparently willing to grant to others provided there was no impingement upon their own practices, and religious *tolerance*, which the Scotch-Irish did not possess.[51] Whatever counties, towns, or villages the Scotch-Irish dominated economically and politically, they expected also to have the greatest religious authority, and they were quick to let outsiders know they were unwelcome.

Some Scotch-Irish Characteristics

From the Scotch-Irishman's religion sprang a number of well known characteristics. One of these is the creed that since everything comes from God, man is obligated to serve him. One aspect of this belief was the Protestant work ethic, which the Scotch-Irish did not invent, though they definitely played their part in developing it. The idea developed because the Puritans and the Scotch-Irish believed that every waking minute should be spent doing something productive; waste of time was sinful. This philosophy affected both rich and poor within the Scotch-Irish community: no one was more revered than a poor person who became wealthy by honest means. Even when one became materially rich, he was still expected to work at something as long as he was physically able. As is well known, many scholars—most notably Max Weber—have made connections between the "Protestant work ethic," and the rise of capitalism in America.[52]

Other characteristics of the Scotch-Irish encouraged by their religious practices included dogmatism, fatalism, and stoicism. The Scotch-Irish had enough *joie de vivre* to overdo things occasionally at fairs, festivals, funerals, wakes and weddings. They were the type of people "kind enough to give someone the shirt off their backs" if they thought that the person needed it more than they; at the same time, however, they would shoot on sight if they had even the slightest idea that someone meant them harm.

By the 1730s, the Scotch-Irish extended all the way from Maine to Pennsylvania. They had made enough enemies by this time (Puritans in New England and Indians and Quakers in Pennsylvania), however, to cause many of them to think once again about moving on. As early as 1727 the Western Pennsylvania Emigrant Society was formed to help those Scotch-Irish who wanted to go west of the Susquehanna River.[53] Another encouragement for western travel was the Pennsylvania government's decision in 1743 not to sell any more lands to the Scotch-Irish in the eastern parts of the colony.[54] The Emigrant Society and governmental strictures were the motivating factors behind the Scotch-Irish move into Adams and York counties, and into the Kittochtinney Valley, today known as Cumberland County.[55]

Lands were cheaper in the west than in the east, and the Scotch-Irish once again showed an adaptability to new areas. Their great forte was apparently in buying land in the west that few other agriculturally minded people wanted, clearing it, and homesteading.

CHAPTER FIVE

Scotch-Irish Moves Into The West

By the 1740s it was generally agreed that "no Scotch-Irish family felt comfortable until it had moved at least twice."[1] From Lowland Scotland to Ulster to America, and then into various parts of the interior, the Scotch-Irish were truly "movers."[2] It must be noted, however, that the Scotch-Irish were not alone in their mobility. James T. Lemon has shown that "many Scotch-Irish settlements persisted where they had begun." Thus "Ulstermen may not have had any more the restlessness often ascribed to them than any other group."[3]

It was the quest for land that caused the Scotch-Irish to travel, first westward out of Lancaster County, Pennsylvania, and then southward through the Cumberland Valley into the Blue Ridge Mountains of Virginia, and ultimately into the Carolinas, upper Georgia, Tennessee, and Kentucky. "They were pioneers of farming in that great swathe of rolling and timbered country stretching from western Maryland and central Pennsylvania south to the Carolinas."[4]

Motives for Moving West

Even many of the Scotch-Irish who had been settled in Pennsylvania for some time decided to join their newly arrived brethren and push into other parts. They had grown disillusioned with the Quaker-dominated Pennsylvania government's soft handling of the Indians, and there had also been some ugly disputes over ownership of lands. One such occurred over a place called Conestoga Manor. James Logan wrote about this problem: "Ye Skirts of Donegal have been so audaciously impudent as to attempt a Settlm't on Conestoga Manor regularly survey'd to the Proprietor's [the Penn family] use almost 15 years since. Some I hear have been so foolishly weak as to value themselves or their number, but they will find themselves mistaken."[5]

Though the Scotch-Irish were largely successful in appropriating the lands of Conestoga Manor and others such as Fagg's Manor,[6] a growing number of them decided to move on to new places where cheap or free land was available in abundance. It was only when the Scotch-Irish came to believe that previously claimed land was being wasted—by being permitted to lie idle, for example—that they moved to make it their own, or at least get the use of it. In the vast majority of cases, the Scotch-Irishman endeavored to get his land in a lawful manner.

Creation of Cumberland County

The inhabitants of the western parts of Lancaster County convinced the colonial authorities that they were too far away from their county seat for it to be of any practical use to them. Thus a new county, Cumberland, was created, made up in part from the already existing Lancaster County. Cumberland's citizens, almost entirely Scotch-Irish, created eighteen townships and gave most of them distinct north Ireland names.[7]

In Cumberland County, the scene of the first great push to the west in Pennsylvania by the Scotch-Irish, there were three legal ways to use land. The first and most desirable was to acquire "patented" land; that is, land for which a deed had been issued and which could be transferred from one owner to another. Second was "warranted" land, which gave the settler permission to survey the plots he wanted, and apply to the government for a patent. "Unwarranted" land remained in the hands of the Commonwealth, though in many instances it was possible for a person to settle on it and grow crops. The greatest number of cases having to do with Scotch-Irish "appropriation" of someone else's property, dealt with "unwarranted" lands.[8]

The Lurgan Township of Cumberland County was created in 1743. William Lynn received 100 acres, and Robert McNut, 200 acres of patented land, while William Jack received fifty unwarranted acres. These three, of course, were among dozens getting land in one form or another in the newly created Cumberland County.

In Fermanagh Township, Alexander Armstrong had the use of 100 unwarranted acres while George Armstrong got 200 acres that were warranted. The Hopewell and Pennsborough townships had been the most westerly of Lancaster County, and became the most easterly of Cumberland County. Widow Andrews received a patent for 170 acres, Francis Campbell for 100 and Janet Miller for fifty, while Benjamin Blythe settled on 400 unwarranted acres.[9]

These examples of land acquisition hinted at the idea that few things were more important to a Scotch-Irishman than ownership of property. Within the living memory of many of these Scotch-Irish rovers was the highly restricted, narrow access to land in the Old World. They certainly did compare the confinements of Ulster to the spaciousness of Pennsylvania. Thus they were awed and entranced not only by the vastness of the land before them, but by its beauty as well. No wonder many of them became diarists, leaving behind graphic descriptions of what they saw.

Some Scotch-Irish Diarists

Though most Scotch-Irish traveled as a family, it is nevertheless true that hundreds of single, unattached young men roamed throughout Pennsylvania and many other parts of the continent as well. One such person was Jonathan Moore (whose voyage across the Atlantic aboard the *Snow Cape Breton* was chronicled in Chapter Three).

He described Philadelphia as "regularity itself" in mid-eighteenth century. It had wide, spacious streets, with houses that were "a medley of stone, bricks, and wood, some high, some low, standing together." The public buildings were "three English, two Presbyterian, one Anabaptist, one Calvinist Dutch, one Lutheran Dutch, one Lutheran Swedish, one Moravian, one Flemish, three Quakers, an academy, a state-house, a townhouse, public hospital, two almshouses, and a workhouse."[10] Philadelphia, Moore said, was only some seventy years old, and its population was already 24,000. "It is a flourishing place, and the province is the best of any in America."[11]

Another Scotch-Irish settler in western Pennsylvania, some fifty miles from Pittsburgh, was Job Johnston, formerly of Slatabogy in Londonderry. He wrote to his brothers, John, Robert, and James, that "It [America] is as good a country as any man dwells in and it is much better than I expected it to be in every way I assure you."[12]

Johnston, like many immigrants, spent a lengthy time in the colonies missing his homeland, and wondering if he had made the right decision by coming over. After about a year, there were no more doubts: "I do not know of one who has come here who desires to be in Ireland again. . . . I have often wondered at our country folk . . . [who] would rather live in slavery and work all the year 'round and not be threepence the better at the year's end." They should, Johnston said, "stir out of their chimney corner," and go to America. But there were many in Ireland, he claimed, "that desire to hear ill of [America], for they would keep their friends there [in Ireland] with them in bondage and slavery."

Johnston's letters home virtually created a textbook of the fauna and flora found in Pennsylvania. He described and discussed bears, wolves, foxes, and rattlesnakes, and spoke glowingly of orchards, "with very limbs torn to pieces with the weight, and most delicious to the taste." He smiled, he said, when he saw clusters of peaches growing on a tree, for they reminded him of onions in the Old Country tied and hanging from a rope. Other fruit he saw in great abundance included apples (from which he drank a "curious" cider), cherries, pears, plums, quinces, strawberries, cranberries, huckleberries, bilberries, gooseberries (which did not grow as well in Pennsylvania as "at home"), currants ("of which the inhabitants make excellent wine"), and grapes. In Pennsylvania, he said, fruit trees destroyed themselves by the very weight of their produce.

As for grain, "where land is good and well laboured, it turns out to admiration." Commonly, each acre produced fifteen to twenty bushels of wheat, but thirty were not unheard of. "Rye grows exceedingly well here," but barley lagged behind. The heat made Pennsylvania a poor place by comparison with Ulster to grow oats, still a staple to the Scotch-Irish just as they had been for centuries in Lowland Scotland. "They [local residents] make no other use . . . [of oats] . . . than to feed their horses. Johnston spoke of a grain called "buckwheat" that was "very good" and of "great service" to both man and beast. "Indian corn [called maize in the Old World] where well vapoured and duly attended will reward the labourers with four or five hundred fold." The ground in Pennsylvania, Johnston said, was easy to till: "A boy and two horses will plow an acre very easy in a day."[13]

Pasturelands were a sight to behold, producing "very fat" cattle, Johnston marveled at farmers giving salt to their cattle. "They tell me it makes them thrive."[14]

Vegetables were in great abundance in western Pennsylvania. Each farmer planted at least two acres of turnips every year, and potatoes (a vegetable dear to the heart of every Scotch-Irishman) did "exceedingly well." Cucumbers, watermelons, "mushmillions," (mushrooms or muskmelons?), and pumpkins were in abundance. "Peas grow very well here, and English beans likewise, but here is beans called kidney that are excellent eating with the podes on."[15]

Johnston feared that his letters would be taken in Ulster as mentioning only the good about America, and omitting all the inconveniences. There was some "barren land," he said, which was true of all countries of the world, and the good land was so much in demand that its price was "commonly" at £6 to £7 an acre. Even with this acquisition of good land, one still could not get anything from it if one chose to be idle. America may have opened a world of opportunities to the Scotch-Irish, but it was a world attendant with hard toil and labor. The shirker would not get very far in colonial America.

Still another Scotch-Irish immigrant, James Murray, wrote home to County Tyrone to the Reverend Baptist Boyd in 1737 that the area around York, Pennsylvania, was a "bonny land." "All things grow here that ever I did see grow in Ereland; and we ha' cows and sheep and Horses plenty here, and Goat and Deers and Raccoons, and Moles and Bever, and Fish and Fowls of all Sorts."[16] The various trades were profitable, too, according to Murray, at least by comparison with the Old Country. A weaver ("wabster") got "twelve pence a yard, a Labourer gets four shillings and six pence a day, a Lass gets four shillings, six pence a week for spinning on the wee wheel, a Carpenter gets six shillings a day and a Tailor gets twenty Shillings for making a suit of Cleaths."[17]

Murray begged the Reverend Boyd to gather up his friends and come to Pennsylvania, and bring with them linen, wool, guns, powder, and shot. God had opened a door for their deliverance, said Murray, and Boyd's two sons, Samuel and James, could earn £100 a year each for their school-teaching abilities. America, Murray declared, regarded a person even of few skills as a "high learned man."

The good Reverend, Murray said, could make a fair living among the settlers "turned Christian;" his congregation would sing the Psalms "bonnily" and "appear to be religious." He claimed that indentured servants had come to York from northern Ireland who, upon ending their servitudes, became "justices of the piece [*sic*]." Murray closed his long letter by asserting that "I will come to Ereland again, the Lord spare me, about two years [hence]," bringing "rum and staves for barrels" and several items to sell to his family and friends.[18]

Scotch-Irish Missing Their "Homes"

Though these Scotch-Irish immigrants were happy to be in Pennsylvania and considered their good fortune to be beyond measure, it is nevertheless true that many, if not most of their letters very frequently used phrases like "back home" (Ireland), and "when I come back." These immigrants deeply missed the family and friends they had left behind, and they harbored resentments against being compelled to leave home in the first place. It took at least a year, sometimes more, for the Scotch-Irish to feel at home in the American colonies; even then, they were apt to retain a longing, romantic image of home somewhere in the Old World.

In all likelihood, however, many of these same Scotch-Irishmen who blamed the English for their transient states would have traveled anyway. They were able to rationalize their material and spiritual existences in the New World by using one or all (economic, religious, climatic), of the adversities they had left behind in the Old. And, of course, the English were usually responsible for the man-made disasters that affected these people. Even if they were not, the image continued to grow among the Scotch-Irish that they were. Thus, the Scotch-Irish hated the English, and all of the institutions (crown, Anglican Church, class systems) asociated with them.

Perhaps it was this yearning for home and at the same time reveling in the wonders of the New World that caused the Scotch-Irish to stick together to such an extent. In all the colonies where they settled the most (Massachusetts, Pennsylvania, Virginia, and the Carolinas), they retained their distinctiveness as an ethnic group, standing ready in most instances to protect and defend one another. This fact remained true at least within distinct villages of Scotch-Irish; on an intercommunity level, the adhesiveness was not so strong.

This collective security had been seen time and again as the Scotch-Irish fought to keep lands they deemed to be more theirs than others. A further example of their banding together for mutual assistance was at Marsh Creek in Adams County, another stronghold of the Scotch-Irish in western Pennsylvania.

In 1741, the Penns wanted a survey to be made of Marsh Creek, presumably with the intention of reserving lands for the proprietary family. The area had already been largely settled by a contingent of the Scotch-Irish, who were not inclined to allow any surveying to be done. Zachariah Butcher was the surveyor, and he wrote of his problems: "I was designed . . . to have laid out the Manor at Marsh Creek but the inhabitants have got into such spirit that it is as much as a man's life is worth to go among them for they gather together in conference and go about armed anytime that I am anywhere near about. They fully resolve to kill or cripple me, or any other persons who shall attempt to lay out a Manor there."[19]

Scotch-Irish Repute Outside Pennsylvania

Accounts such as this one spread rapidly throughout the Pennsylvania colony and bolstered the Scotch-Irish reputation as one of boldness, audacity, and hard-headed rigidity. Indeed, their reputation went far beyond Pennsylvania's borders. Lord Baltimore in Maryland, wanting (among other things) increased protection against Indians, offered 200 acres to families and 100 acres to individuals free of rent for three years.[20] This was a general offer to all colonists in America, and the Scotch-Irish were among the first to take advantage of it.

Virginia, even more than Maryland, felt the need for some buffer between the Indians in the western parts of the colony and the more populated areas of the east. Thus, the Scotch-Irish were welcomed into the Great Valley, but they came only after Virginia Governor George Gooch assured the Presbyterian Synod of Philadelphia that they would not be hindered in their religious practices and beliefs.

Ths Scotch-Irish pushed across the Susquehanna River and followed the arc of the mountains that acted somewhat as a barrier for further westward expansion but furnished easy access to the valleys, to Virginia, and to the Carolinas.[21]

Generally, in their move southward, the Scotch-Irish followed the Great Philadelphia Wagon Road.[22] Parke Rouse noted that Market Street in Philadelphia has been called "the most historical highway" in America, for from it, "the Great Philadelphia Wagon Road eventually led southward into the American heartland."[23]

Starting in Philadelphia, the road went to Lancaster and York, and crossed the Potomac River into the Shennandoah Valley at Williams's Ferry. Then it ran south through Winchester, Stephensburg, Strasburg, and Staunton, crossing the James River at Looney's Ferry (now Buchanon, West Virginia), and then swung south to Roanoke. From there it headed east through the Staunton River gap of the Blue Ridge Mountains, then south along the mountains, going across the Blackwater, Pigg, Irwine, and Dan to a terminus at Wachovia, in North Carolina. From here the Scotch-Irish, and, of course, other immigrant groups, spread out even further into South Carolina areas known as the "New Mesopotamia," between the Yadkin and Catawba Rivers.[24]

Off the wagon road at various points were "wilderness trails" going west into Tennessee and Kentucky. Some Scotch-Irish took these trails, but the vast majority stayed on the wagon road. (It was just before, during, and just after the American Revolution that the Scotch-Irish came in any number to Tennessee and Kentucky).

The House Diary

Thousands of people, of course, used the Great Philadelphia Wagon Road at least for parts of their journeys into the interior. One such person was Elizabeth House, later to become Mrs. Nicholas Trist, who traveled from Philadelphia to Louisiana in the 1780s. She continued over the mountains into the Pittsburgh area, leaving the wagon road when it turned south at York.

Miss House spoke of the conditions of houses where they stayed. Her descriptions ranged all the way from "I believe if there are good people in the world they are to be found at this place'' to ''I don't believe any of the children had been washed since they were born; I had no idea that there were such beings upon this earth.''[25]

She gave an insight into the difficulties sometimes encountered by a single woman traveling alone. On the trail, it was customary for men and women, especially in cold weather, to sleep overnight in the same room. Though she went along with this custom, Elizabeth refused to let anyone see her while she prepared for bed at night, and then dressed the next morning. One woman in her company chided Elizabeth for her modesty, and said that she thought ''a woman must be very insecure in herself that was afraid to sleep in the room with a strange man.'' The woman saw nothing ''indelicate'' in the matter, for ''no man wou'd take a liberty with a woman unless he saw a disposition in her to encourage him.''[26] After several weeks on the road Elizabeth got safely to Louisiana, where she ultimately married Nicholas Trist, and became the mother of the well-known statesman and diplomat.

Hastings Diary

Sally Hastings was another traveler west in Pennsylvania. In a group of ten persons she struck out from Lancaster for Washington, Pennsylvania, some 250 miles away. She gave this description of being in Dauphin County:

''After traveling . . . through very swampy roads, occasioned by the late excessive rains, we arrived late last night at an Inn. We were quite Spiritless. . . . We were likewise disturbed by the noise of an intoxicated Gentleman.'' Sally was only eighteen miles from her home, but already she became philosophical about her departure: ''I begin to perceive that the links of the chain which bind man to man are become exceedingly fragile.''[27]

Crossing the Susquehanna, Sally had such fear of the ferry that ''it required a full quarter of an hour's Reasoning to convince me, that, to a Predestinarian, the greatest Danger, and no Danger, is absolutely the same thing!'' She seemed to sum up much of mankind's experience itself when she exclaimed, ''Perhaps there are no two things in Nature more at variance, than my Principles and Practice.''[28]

Cumberland County was ''fine champaign country, in the highest state of cultivation, here and there interspersed with decadent Farm-houses.'' The surrounding mountains rose like ''smoky columns,'' and lost their ''azure summits amidst the fleeting clouds.'' Despite the physical beauty around her, Sally found the people in Carlisle to ''possess an air of impertinent curiosity.'' She became somewhat snobbish herself as she wrote, ''One of the misfortunes of Travellers . . . [is] . . . that their Situation excludes them in a great Measure, from the Society of those who are generally styled 'the better Sort,' and consequently, their Observations are, for the most part, confined to the Populace.''[29]

In Franklin County, Sally found the land poor, the houses little better than huts, but the inhabitants ''appear to be well-informed.'' She marveled at the pine trees in Franklin County, which grew ''exceedingly tall and beautiful'' and ''retained their verdure through all the severity of winter.'' She liked the little town of Shippensburg, a mile in length, and consisting of one street, with many good houses. Sally went on to behold a mountain whose grandeur forced into insignificance ''all the works of art'' she had ever seen, and she loved staying at Fannetsburg in the Path Valley in the midst of the Blue Ridge Mountains.[30] Her descriptions, plus many more that were written, attested that the Scotch-Irish did have an eye for natural beauty whenever they saw it, even to the point sometimes of romanticizing it. They were not solely the stern people that they have frequently been depicted as being.

Spreading Into the Wilderness Areas

Several hundred Scotch-Irish continued over the mountains into extreme western Pennsylvania, and from there ultimately into Indiana, Kentucky, and Tennessee. By the thousands, however, they turned left at the mountains and went to Virginia and the Carolinas.

While the Scotch-Irish were welcome in these parts by governors and other officials because of their hostility to the Indians, good opinions of them were not universally shared. Unfortunately, the Scotch-Irish reputation preceded their actual arrival, and made many already established residents to be quite wary of them.

Grumpy old William Byrd likened the immigration of the Scotch-Irish from Pennsylvania to the invasion of the Goths and Vandals in ancient history.[31] The worst criticisms, however, came from an Anglican clergyman, Charles Woodmason. They were "very poor," he said, "owing to their extreme Indolence." And then he got worse: "They delight in Their present, low, lazy, sluttish, heathenish, hellish life, and seem not desirous of changing it. Both men and women will do anything to come at Liquor, Cloaths, furniture . . . rather than work for it."[32] Some of their more serious vices Woodmason listed as licentiousness, wantonness, lasciviousness, rudeness, lewdness, and profligacy. He said they "lived wholly on Butter, Milk, Clabber, and what in England is given to Hogs and Dogs."[33]

At least for Woodmason, things did not get any better. He later described the dividing line between North and South Carolina as the "finest body" of land to be seen anywhere. Unfortunately, at least from his viewpoint, it was occupied by a "Sett of the most lowest vilest crew breathing—Scotch-Irish Presbyterians from the North of Ireland." To make things worse, their pastor, the Reverend William Richardson, was a former Anglican, but became a Presbyterian over a dispute he had with the Church of England. Woodmason depicted him as a "captive" of his Presbyterian congregations who could do little (such as saying the Lord's Prayer or using Watt's Psalms) without permission.[34]

For their part, the offended Scotch-Irish struck back at Woodmason. They changed the preaching notices that the Reverend posted on his door, and deliberately gave wrong directions to people making their way to his church. Sometimes they lurked outside the church before services and gave quantities of whiskey to the congregation, and frequently got many of them quite drunk. Once, the Scotch-Irish set fifty-seven dogs to fighting during a church service. Woodmason "caught one bitch, took it to a deacon's house, and slyly intimated that it was one of the fifty-seven Presbyterians he had just converted."[35]

Augusta County, Virginia

The Scotch-Irish were hard-headed as well as physically strong (as, indeed, were most of the other colonists); thus, they could sustain attacks from the likes of Woodmason and penetrate into the frontier areas. The first major clustering of the Scotch-Irish in Virginia was in Augusta County, the principal city of which became Staunton (later the birthplace of President Woodrow Wilson, a Scotch-Irish descendant).

John Lewis, a refugee from Ulster, was probably the first Scotch-Irishman to settle in the Upper Shenandoah Valley.[36] When his landlord back in Ireland had tried to take his home from him, Lewis killed the landlord, and fled to America. At first harried by the law, but later exonerated on grounds of self-defense, Lewis settled in the "Irish tract" of Augusta County, on the headwaters of the South Fork of the Shenandoah River. In time he greatly prospered and built one of the finest estates, "Bellefonte," to be found anywhere in Virginia. On his gravestone he directed to be written: "Here lies the remains of John Lewis, who slew the Irish Lord, settled in Augusta County, located the town of Staunton, and furnished five sons to fight the battles of the American Revolution."[37]

Augusta County Court

By 1745 a civil court existed in Augusta County, and its function was more secular than the church courts that had operated in Pennsylvania. It dealt more with clearly civil and criminal offenses than with religious matters. Apparently, however, this civil court embodied as well the ecclesiastical infractions that frequently occurred in Scotch-Irish Presbyterian churches.

Robert Young, for example, brought a woman into Augusta County, whose support was likely to be charged to his parish. Young was ordered by the court to explain his activities. There were many orders for "titheables" (those people belonging to local churches) to work on roads and do river maintenance.[38] The court also issued or denied building permits, certificates for the cultivation of hemp (out of which rope was made), and appointed inspectors of beef and pork that were to be sold to the public.[39] In these activities, the court assumed a "good stewardship policy," believing that its main function was to protect the public weal. This stance made it somewhat different from church courts that operated elsewhere in the country.[40]

There were enough enquiries into parishioners' private lives, however, to give this court an ecclesiastical character. Patrick Savage was hailed before it to show why his children should not be "bound out" (that is, placed in foster homes) because he appeared incapable "of bringing them up in a Christian-like manner." James Shekelford was indicted for swearing, and James O'Neil for a breach of the sabbath. These were just three of the innumerable cases showing the power and influence of the Augusta County Court.[41]

Physical punishment was often meted out to offenders. John Dunn, convicted of larceny, got thirty-nine lashes of the whip. Mary Wolfinger was convicted of a felony, but her husband appealed to the court, unsuccessfully, to administer the twenty-lash punishment to him. Other matters with which the court dealt included horsestealing, fighting, runaway slaves, jail breaks, and quarrels between the white settlers and native Indians.[42]

In the Augusta County court records exist many notices by citizens that they intended to leave the colony, usually to go to Carolina. One wonders if the court's permission to leave was necessary for those individuals who wanted to travel. In all likelihood, the permissions showed that the would-be traveler had cleared outstanding debts and obligations; for a Scotch-Irishman to ask any government, local or otherwise, for permission to leave a place would have been distinctly out of character.

Into the Carolinas

A decade after the move into Virginia, settlers, predominantly Scotch-Irish, poured into the area between the sandy plains of the east and the Blue Ridge Mountains in the west known as the Carolina piedmont. They traveled in Conestoga wagons, "the vehicles of empire."[43] Their motives for going to Carolina were the traditional ones of acquiring free or cheap lands.

Conflicts arose in many instances when the Scotch-Irish tried to claim some of the North Carolina lands. A goodly part of North Carolina was still claimed by proprietary families and also by the crown. Unscrupulous land agents did a boom business by selling lands they knew to be the object of prior claims. When word spread about the agents, the Scotch-Irish settlers relied upon their time-tested method of getting land—appropriations unto themselves. "Many Scotch-Irishmen who had neither the means nor the education to combat the corrupt officials simply selected a desirable tract and squatted."[44] Eventually, the colonial government in North Carolina passed laws giving squatters an opportunity to buy lands they had already preempted. In most cases, the settler made arrangements to buy the land.

One of the earliest major Scotch-Irish landholders in North Carolina was Henry McCulloch. In 1736 he secured a grant from George II for 64,000 acres in Duplin County in the southeast part of North Carolina. He ultimately settled 322 immigrants, "young and old," from Ulster.[45] Besides the McCullochs, another prominent Scotch-Irish family in North Carolina was that of Archibald Houston, who came from Anson (later Mecklenburg) County. He received large grants of land upon which he allowed less wealthy Scotch-Irishmen to make their livings.

And there were plenty of less wealthy Scotch-Irishmen. By the 1750s owners of ships were advertising heavily for passengers, and one was the *Elizabeth*, headed for Charlestown (Charleston) and Wilmington, commanded by Captain Nathaniel Sayer. Readers of the *Belfast Newsletter* were advised that "this new colony of North Carolina lies in the most temperate latitudes. No excessive colds or heats are ever felt. . . . All sorts of European grain survives in a surprising manner as well as flax and hemp, potatoes, and fruits of all kinds." There was a "hardy welcome" in the Carolinas for "all industrious strangers." Especially needed were carpenters, joiners, smiths, shoemakers, and millwrights. If a person wanted to go as an indentured servant, he would work for a stipulated time for Captain Sayer, and then receive fifty acres, two cows, ten hogs, a gun, and a winter suit of clothes.[46] Another Carolina-bound ship was the *Dobb's Galley*, sponsored by the North Carolina governor himself.

According to one historical study, however, the Scotch-Irish may have had a reason other than land acquisition for going into the Carolinas. The Scotch-Irish, wrote Forrest McDonald and Grady McWhiney, brought with them to the New World the Scottish Lowland practice of open range for their livestock, including hogs.[47] Even the lowest peasant could run his swine over the uncultivated lands of wealthy nobility. In the South, from 1715 to 1837, McDonald and McWhiney claim, "the hog was king," and corn the predominant crop.[48] Thus, "hog drives" became well known in the colonial South, producing quite large fortunes for numerous drivers, and creating "hog roads" and "hog hotels." Sometimes the hogs numbered as many as 1,000 per mile as they moved out of North Carolina to ports like Charleston and Savannah and to large southern cities like Richmond and Baltimore.[49]

South Carolina

South Carolina, in the "Mesopotamian" area between the Yadkin and Catawba Rivers, was the first southern terminus for those Scotch-Irish and their descendants who had moved out of Pennsylvania. As in most instances, the Scotch-Irish went into South Carolina to acquire land, and to get away from "intruding civilizations."

The primary route for the Scotch-Irish from Pennsylvania to the south was through Winchester and Staunton, in Virginia; Salem and Salisbury, in North Carolina; and Lancaster and Florence, in South Carolina. A secondary route brought settlers from Pennsylvania to Williamsburg, Virginia, through Halifax, North Carolina—the so-called "Chesapeake Route," or "Trading Path"—to what is today the Winston-Salem area.

In time, the port of Charlestown became almost as important as Philadelphia in receiving Scotch-Irishmen from the Old World. These latecomers, arriving from the 1760s on, usually went first to the North Carolina piedmont, and then worked their way to Georgia, which at that time included Alabama territory. Cheap cotton lands drew the Scotch-Irish into these localities in the deep South. From Georgia and Alabama many Scotch-Irish made their way into Tennessee.

Tennessee and Kentucky

The vast majority of Scotch-Irishmen, however, came into Tennessee by way of the Cumberland Gap from Kentucky. Once in Tennessee, they settled primarily in Davidson, Montgomery, Sumner, and Maury Counties.

The Scotch-Irish in Kentucky derived from departures along the "Great Philadelphia Wagon Road" into numerous wilderness treks, and through the Cumberland Gap from Tennessee. By 1763 there had been so many immigrants, primarily Scotch-Irish, crossing the Appalachians and appropriating Indian lands that Parliament created a "proclamation line" to prohibit any further white settlement west of the mountains.

The "proclamation line" was a failure; it would have taken the entire British army to enforce it. Frontiersmen like Daniel Boone blazed pathways that later became major transportation routes, with so many people coming into the area that in 1792

Kentucky had more than enough population to qualify it for statehood.

The areas of Kentucky predominantly settled by Scotch-Irish were in the north central parts of the state, around Lexington, Georgetown, and Richmond. Travelers lavished praise upon the land that later became the Blue Grass State: "The face of this country [Kentucky] was . . . delightful beyond conception. Nearly one half of it was covered with cane, and between the brakes spaces of open ground as if intended by nature for open fields. The ground appeared extremely fertile and produced amazing quantities of reeds of various kinds, wild grass, wild rye, and clover. The dews were very heavy, the nights in the heat of summer cool."[50]

Another settler rhapodized: "The land that we passed over today is like a paradise. It is so good and beautiful. The land is so good that I cannot give it its due praise. Its undergrowth is clover, cane, peavine, and nettles, intermixed with rich weed. Its timber is honey locust, black walnut, sugar tree hickory, iron wood, hoopwood, mulberry, ash and elm, and some oak."[51]

The Scotch-Irish: A Summary

From Massachusetts in the north to South Carolina in the south and Kentucky in the west, the Scotch-Irish became a factor in populating the North American continent. Of course, every state has its own contingent of Scotch-Irish,[52] but the predominance lay in New England, Pennsylvania, and the South. Approximately 250,000 Scotch-Irish came to America during the colonial period. By the early 1990s, there were some 20 million descendants of those early settlers.

Though there is today no distinctive ethnic group in North America known as the "Scotch-Irish," at least in the sense that they congregate in specific rural or urban localities, there is nevertheless a strong identification with the historical Scotch-Irish. This identification undoubtedly plays a role in determining the traits, characteristics, and even opinions of millions of Americans.

By 1760 the settlement patterns of the Scotch-Irish had been fairly well set. Though the entry ports stayed busy receiving immigrants from Ulster, there did not seem to be any new interior territories they were interested in obtaining. The Scotch-Irish from Maine to Georgia went about their business of working small farms, growing wheat, corn, cotton, and some tobacco. They enjoyed the bounty of the New World so much that they became determined that no one would ever take it away from them. This attitude became crucial in a few years' time, when the American Revolution was just in the making.

CHAPTER SIX

Scotch-Irish Ways Of Life

By the middle of the 18th century, the Scotch-Irish personified the American frontiersmen, having strong and pointed opinions about the world and their place in it. As they pushed into the western parts the Scotch-Irish were a mixture of settlers who were generations removed from those first Ulster immigrants and new arrivals who continued to flood the ports of New York, Charleston, New Castle, and, especially, Philadelphia. Whether old or new, however, they possessed the same system of value expressed in religion, education, lifestyles, and attitudes toward warfare.

RELIGION

Practical Qualities

Despite the Scotch-Irish propensity for religious dogmatism, from the 1740s on all was not well within the framework of their beloved Presbyterianism. They were expected to conform to rules and regulations emanating from the Philadelphia synod in reference to doctrines of predestination and the elect. Ultimately, however, their fierce independence drove many

Scotch-Irish away from a system they increasingly deemed to be "cold, dead, and formalistic."[1] They wanted to instill some emotionalism and subjective responses into their religion; thus, large numbers of Scotch-Irish drifted into other denominations such as the Baptists and Methodists, while others hoped to reform Presbyterianism to accommodate their wishes. The Old Side Presbyterians wanted to retain the historic functioning of their church; they were "committed to creeds and dogmas and fearful of change or adaptation to the American frontier environment."[2] The New Side favored emotional conversions and spiritual enthusiasm[3] during their services, and revivalism.

There was undoubtedly a link between the formation of New Side Presbyterianism and the settling of western parts by the Scotch-Irish. On the frontier, there was little need for finely spun theories, either political or religious. The "workability" factor required that a religious service, including the sermon, "do something" for the frontiersmen. They had to be made to feel personally good about their religion instead of adhering to corporate doctrines that had been formulated elsewhere. The New Side seemed more tied to forms of populism than the Old Side, and to some extent its revivals were of Old World origins. Marilyn J. Westerkamp, in *Triumph of the Laity*, said: "It cannot be coincidental that outbreaks of revivalism in Pennsylvania and New Jersey followed directly after large-scale migration from Ireland, nor that the [Great] Awakening spread to Virginia and the Carolina back country during the years when the Scots-Irish moved south."[4] (The Great Awakening was a religious movement primarily in the 1740s which, through a series of revivals, sought to restore some of the conservative Calvinist philosophies thougnt to have been threatened by a few changes in, among other things, the covenant systems by which the Puritans had always governed their religion).

Work of Some New Siders

The Tennent family in Pennsylvania were the leaders of New Side Presbyterianism in the Great Awakening. William Tennent, a native of Armagh, did not like the "discipline of bishops," and his son Gilbert, "advocated evanagelical piety rather than intellectual learning."[5] While the Tennents were leaders in New Side theology and education, they were not alone in their endeavors, as the work of people like Alexander Craighead attests.

Alexander Craighead, pastor of the Middle Octorara Presbyterian Church in Pennsylvania, defined in 1743 much of the New Side philosophy. (Later, Craighead took his doctrines to Virginia and to Sugaw Creek in North Carolina, where "he called down brimstone and hell-fire on sinners.")[6]

He quarreled with the American Presbyterian Synod's failure to abandon the crown as the head of the church. Charles II, Craighead maintained, had committed a "heaven daring" and "God provoking" sin by allowing his parliament to "burn our holy covenants" through the Test Act.[7] King William was guilty of "treachery and deceit" because he sat "in the place of God" and usurped "Christ's royal prerogative" by declaring himself as the head of the Presbyterian Church. George I, claimed Craighead, was a Lutheran, thereby having no right to rule over Presbyterian doctrine. Likewise, George II did not embrace the "true faith," being instead the "protector of sectarian heretics."[8]

Craighead also objected to the Old Side practice of offering communion to all "they believe to have grace" and who professed Christianity. He apparently wanted to restrict this ordinance to those members of the "antipopish, antiLutheran, antriprelatic, antiErastian, antilatitudinarian, antisectarian, true Presbyterian Church of Christ in America."[9] Leaving no stone unturned, the good reverend added that it was his duty to speak out against heresies and schisms like "independency, libertinism, anbaptism, antinomianism, Arminianism, Socinianism, Quakerism, Erastianism, Deism, Moravianism, and that awful error . . . [of] . . . Catholicism."[10]

Craighead claimed, as did indeed many of the Old Siders, still to adhere to the Calvinistic doctrines set forth in the Westminster Confession of Faith, adopted by Scottish Presbyterians in August, 1647. According to Craighead this Confession, however, did not negate the covenants of the 1630s, that had bound Presbyterians together in the face of religious persecution from the English church and crown. Some Presbyterian ministers in America, Craighead argued, denied the effect of those covenants, which, among other things, recognized God—not the crown—as the head of the church. Those denials, Craighead believed, constituted another reason for breaking with formal Presbyterianism.

Craighead's dissents did not go unnoticed by the Presbyterian hierarchy. (Ranked from bottom to top the hierarchy was: church, presbytery, synod, General Assembly.) The Donegal Presbytery accused him of absenteeism, imposing new terms of communion (such as excluding anyone who did not profess New Side beliefs), and of asserting that, contrary to this presbytery's rules, a minister ought not to be restricted to just one congregation.[11] His battles with the authorities caused Craighead to quit Pennsylvania and go to the frontier, where his New Side proclivities were widely accepted. Even in the wilderness, however, Craighead got into trouble. Two members of his Augusta County, Virginia, congregation complained that he "maintained treasonable positions, though they offered no definitions. Virginia governor Robert Dinwiddie ordered the Augusta County sheriff to take Craighead into custody and bring him to Williamsburg. In the capital, Craighead took a loyalty oath to the crown, and was returned to his pulpit.[12] He left Virginia, however, and moved on to North Carolina.

Work of John Craig and Joseph Rhea

Craighead's New Side philosophies were, in a way, an index to the times with respect to Protestant Christianity. For each New Side argument, an Old Side rebuttal could always be found. John Craig, an Old Sider, publicly protested the "ruin of church government" by the New Siders, causing a few families in his congregation to regard him as "an opposer of the word of God."[13] The clergy, in general, said Craig, had come into "lowly circumstances" throughout the entire country, in part because of the Old Side-New Side controversy. Among other things, the "reproach of greed" was frequently cast upon preachers. For that reason, Craig never demanded a stipend for marriage or filling vacancies, though he did accept bounties whenever offered.[14]

Another Old Sider, the Reverend Joseph Rhea, detested the "wild enthusiasm faction" which has arisen in the Presbyterian Church.[15] Superstition and bigotry were the by-products of the New Side theology, Rhea claimed, and "unquestionably destructive to true and undefiled religion."[16]

Some Observers of Religious Controversies

The quarrels among the clergy intensified lay attitudes and opinions about Christianity. Diarist Jonathan Moore (discussed previously in Chapters Three and Five) noted that he had heard revivalist George Whitefield preach. Of him, Moore said, "never did I hear words so emphatical by the power of oratory. He preaches in the Presbyterian Church [Moore did not say whether Old Side or New Side] and denominations seem very fond of him. Yet, I don't hear that he encourages or intimates that people should quit the churches they belong to, or form separate meetings. . . ."[17]

Whitefield, however, was accused by many of being a demagogic revivalist who did try to convert people away from their old religious denominations. Charles Chauncy, an avid anti-revivalist, claimed that Whitefield was "the grand promoter of all the confusion there has been in the land."[18]

Preacher arguments, said Moore, had driven the American colonies toward secularism. In Pennsylvania, he said, the appearance of religion was not as great as in New England, but he believed true Christianity still to exist in Penn's colony. Maryland was mixed, he claimed; some parts were Christian, some were not. Virginia had less Christianity than Maryland, and North Carolina less than Virginia. South Carolina was a small improvement over North Carolina, but then came Georgia, which was practically devoid of any religion. "In short," he snorted, "the generality of people in the southern provinces" is that they "are polite heathens."[19] The worst part of this "low ebb" of Christianity, said Moore, was that slaveholders "entirely neglected" to have their slaves instructed in the Christian faith. Also, proselyting efforts were at a minimum among the Indians, leaving them "wicked and debauched," without the "civilizing" benefits of Christianity.[20]

Another lay observer of the American scene was Jane Smith, who wrote several descriptive letters to the Weir family in County Tyrone, north Ireland. "Religion in this country . . . seems greatly on the decline." By the 1770s, Jane claimed, the New Siders were refusing to honor much of the Old Testament, which was, of course, a standby of Calvinistic persuasions. The Old Testament saints, she ascribed the New Siders as believing, "knew nothing of our Redeemer." She spoke of the revivals that were popular in the back country, especially Kentucky. "No doubt you have heard of them," she wrote William Weir, "fainting and falling down, working in fits, and whenever they come to exhorting and praying for hours together."[21] Some revivalists, Jane said, went so far as to say that they were as pure as Adam and Eve, and walked around the meetings naked. "Some say they actually did so," Jane closed her letter, "but I will not affirm it for truth."[22]

Margaret Duncan, another Scotch-Irish immigrant, wrote to members of the Weir family back in Ireland. She lamented the condition of religion in New York. "The morals of the young generation and indeed many of the old is greatly corrupted." Deism, Margaret believed, was a great threat to "true" religion. Its practice "prevails much among us so that we are much worse than this city [New York] was twenty years agone."[23]

Influences of the Religious Controversies

Despite the quarrels among the clergy and the uncertainties affecting the laity, there were still many accomplishments by Scotch-Irish dominated Presbyterian churches during the middle to late eighteenth century. Both the Old Sider and New Sider remained greatly concerned about his personal relationship with God.[24] Also, circuit riders continued to penetrate into the most remote wilderness areas, bringing messages of religious hope to secluded backwood settlements. These Presbyterian preachers were adept at impromptu services, continuing a tradition that had begun during the convenanting days in Scotland and Ireland.[25] Many pastors took sabbaticals from their congregations to preach for extended periods in the frontier areas. And many Presbyterians stipulated that young would-be ministers could not be ordained until they had spent a considerable time administering to the religious wishes of wilderness settlers.[26] Thus, as one author put it, "Religion, in its deepest meaning, was of the very marrow of their [Scotch-Irish] existence and had much indeed to do . . . with their pursuit of material well-being, with the structure of their social and community life, and above all with their moral stance, their socio-political attitudes, and their political activities."[27]

Many religious practices were changed because of the New Side-Old Side conflict. One was that congregations increasingly elected the ministers they wanted to serve them. A bias was created against college-educated preachers in favor of those who were "called" to the pulpit. The congregational ministerial elections soon overlapped into ideas that perhaps more people than before should be involved in the election of public officials. Thus, the Presbyterian conflicts helped to produce a representative concept in America that had significance in the years ahead. As one author put it, the controversy made people aware that "dogmatism and authority were not always perfect persuaders."[28]

The controversies helped to create concepts of evangelism, not only among Presbyterians, but many other Protestant denominations as well. Religious groups found that if they were going to survive, they had to reflect the moods of the times. Since expansion into wilderness areas and pragmatic ideas were the essence of middle to late eighteenth century life in America, denominations that once were rigid found they had to change. The Presbyterians were at the center of these upheavals and moved from being one of the most conservative bodies in the early eighteenth century to libral practices of congregational power in the closing years of that century. It was fitting that the Presbyterian Church became a "mover," in much the same manner as the thousands of Scotch-Irish it represented.[29]

EDUCATION

Erudite Ministers

In many ways, though they would not easily admit it, the Scotch-Irish Presbyterians were similar to the Puritans. Religious dogmatism certainly was one similarity, but the greatest was the shared belief in acquiring at least a modicum of education. Literacy was encouraged so that one could become familiar with the scriptures. Religion and education were so closely intertwined in the Scotch-Irish system of values that frequently it was difficult to distinguish between them.

At least until the Old Side-New Side controversy, there was often a decided difference between the laity and clergy in levels of education. The Old Side, for example, demanded a "European university degree as a qualification for the ministry."[30] The frontiersmen sought enough education to be able to read the Bible, to write to maintain diaries and correspondence, and "ciphering" to keep account books. Both urban and rural Presbyterians, like other citizens of the time, did not bother themselves with too many philosophical niceties. They had to take care of their day-to-day problems without too much contemplation of the universe.

The Presbyterian clergy, however, were quite an erudite lot. Many were graduates of the Universities of Glascow and Edinburgh, and while they may have come to America to administer to the spiritual needs of common, ordinary folk, they nevertheless brought an intense intellectual curiosity with them.

The Reverend Joseph Rhea had been the pastor of Fahan and other churches in County Donegal, North Ireland, before coming to America in 1769. He, like many of his colleagues, had a lengthy correspondence around the country, most of it in Latin. He was interested in planetary movements, the Ptolemaic system, and the philosophies of Plato and Aristotle, and he seemed thoroughly fascinated by ocean tides.[31]

John Craig was a "Mess John" or divinity student at Glascow who spent from 10 June to 17 August 1734 traveling from Larne to Newcastle. He lived for some time in Philadelphia, then went to Augusta County, Virginia, where he taught school for a year and then "read" (studied the scriptures) for two years. Thus, Craig made significant contributions not only to Protestant Christianity in the North American colonies, but to the development of education as well.[32]

The schools in which Craig and others taught were usually crude log cabins, where the benches and tables were made of split logs. Sometimes the community church doubled as a school,[33] and frequently in the warmer climes "field schools" operated. Much depended upon the headmaster or headmistress to see that good teaching and learning took place. Very often, school teachers became important members of the community where they carried out their craft.

Much stress was placed in these schools upon the Bible, both the Old and New Testaments. After religious studies, reading, writing, and arithmetic were seen to. Generally, the school sessions were all day, unless the students were required to be at home for gathering certain crops such as corn or tobacco. These early backwoods schools instilled the thought that "only an educated people could be free."[34]

Higher Education

In addition to creating lower schools, the Scotch-Irish laid much of the groundwork for higher education in America, and in this respect, William Tennent, leader of New Side Presbyterianism in the Great Awakening, was most important. Tennent was a cousin of James Logan, the Penns's secretary. Logan gave Tennent fifty acres on Neshaminy Creek in Bucks County, Pennsylvania, in 1726.[35] Here, he built a school that came to be called the "log college." Ultimately, several of these log colleges were created.

Theology was first among the subjects taught at the log colleges. Tennent himself, who became known as "Hell Fire Tennent,"[36] taught this subject to his students. After theology the log college curriculum stressed Greek, Latin, and Arts and Sciences. Some of the colleges even showed concern for historical knowledge. By this time the Scotch-Irish had an estimable history, and they taught it as a way of exemplifying the idea that freedoms generally come to a people only after many hard struggles. Besides, it was a good way to denigrate their old enemy, Roman Catholicism.

The first graduates of Tennent's log college included three of his own sons, and Samuel and John Blair, Samuel Finley, Charles Beatty, and John Rowland. J. B. Woodburn said of Tennent's log college: "It did a great work and helped to lay the foundations of American intellectual life."[37]

Inspired by Tennent's log college movement, numerous other colleges and universities were founded through Scotch-Irish efforts. Perhaps the most notable was Princeton University in New Jersey, which opened in April, 1747, in the home of Jonathan Dickinson of Elizabeth.[38] Others in Pennsylvania included Dickinson College, Washington and Jefferson, Allegheny College, Lafayette, Grove City, Beaver, Wilson, Waynesboro College, and the Universities of Pittsburgh and Pennsylvania. Some institutions outside Pennsylvania were Hampden-Sidney College in Virginia, University of Virginia, and the University of North Carolina. One historian has claimed that "of the 207 permanent colleges founded before 1861, well over half were established by Presbyterians and New Englanders."[39] In addition to William Tennent, Francis Alison was another important personality in the development of American higher education. He came from County Donegal in Ulster, and was a graduate of Glascow University. In 1744 he founded the New London Academy in Delaware. In time it became Newark College, and still later, the University of Delaware. Alison taught at least three future signers of the American Declaration of Independence and Charles Thomson, in whose handwriting the Declaration was first presented to the Continental Congress.[40]

Though Scotch-Irish colleges were founded primarily to train ministers, in time they took on the dual role of also teaching political and economic philosophies. These colleges definitely played their part in teaching students to resist governmental tyrannies, teachings that were not lost on the generation which would make the American Revolution.

LIFESTYLES

Settling Into Communities

While it is true that many thousands of Scotch-Irish lived in large cities in America (particularly Boston and Philadelphia), they increasingly came to be identified with the frontier. Frequently, a Scotch-Irish family traveled overland, either by wagon or on foot, for several weeks to free wilderness land they could claim as their own.

A Scotch-Irish newcomer into a community usually wore leather or woolen trousers, leather moccasins, a linsey shirt, a deerskin coat,[41] and a hat made from the skin of a raccoon. These frontiersmen depended on woodland animals for both food and clothing. The Scotch-Irishman's children also dressed in wool and leather garments in winter and linsey-woolsey (a thin garment made of linen and wool or cotton and wool) in summer. His wife, however, was apparently more scantily attired. North Carolina Governor Arthur Dobbs, reported in 1755 after a trip to the piedmont that he "found no woman wearing more than one shift and one thin petticoat."[42] He did not elaborate on how he came by this knowledge.

The first duty of a Scotch-Irishman upon arrival in a new neighborhood was to provide housing for himself and family.

Though in Pennsylvania, Scotch-Irish houses were frequently built of rock, in the manner of Ulster, small log structures fit their needs on the frontier. The frontier was constantly expanding, and the Scotch-Irish moved with it. Thus, shelters that were relatively easy to construct and abandon became the preferred type.[43]

Ordinarily, most able-bodied people in a settlement turned out to help the newcomer put up his cabin; the "log-raising" became an important social function on the frontier. First came the felling of trees and hewing them into shape for construction. By dinnertime (the noonday meal), the first story of the house would be completed. By suppertime (the evening meal), the structure would be ready for occupancy.

The women cooked elaborate meals which frequently featured wild game such as deer, fowl, and turkey, accompanied by fried mush with wild honey, pone bread (made of corn, or maize), succotash, johnny-cakes, potatoes, and turnips.[44] And, always, there were the inevitable jugs of whiskey. One visitor to a newly created Scotch-Irish homestead exclaimed: "I believe I saw more peaches and apples rotting on the ground than would sink the British fleet. I was at many plantations in Ohio where they no more knew the number of their hogs than myself. . . . the poorest families adorn their table three times a day like a wedding dinner—tea, coffee, beef, fowls, pies, eggs, pickles, and good bread."[45]

As the house went up, young boys dug a "mortar hole" in which they mixed clay and water for the chinking.[46] (However, in some churches, chinking was purposefully omitted, so the worshipers could keep an eye out for the approach of any unfriendly Indians). The only nails used in these log cabins were to hold down the roof; all the logs were dovetailed together. Each log cabin generally had one room downstairs where the family cooked, ate, sewed, prepared seed for planting, and spun cloth, and one room upstairs for sleeping. There were no partitions in either of these rooms. The cabins seldom had windows, and only a few had other than dirt floors.[47] A chimney, as one author put it, became a status symbol.[48] Poor settlers (who constituted the majority) had to make do with wooden chimneys daubed over with lime. The better-to-do settlers built brick chimneys, obviously more efficient and safe than the wooden ones.

Most settlers, however, both poor and rich, tended to view their log cabins as temporary expedients. If they did not move on to some new frontier, these people wanted permanent residences made of brick. The log cabins in which they started out, they converted into shelters for their cattle, or if they were slave-holders, quarters for their slaves.[49]

The nature of the Scotch-Irish existence turned them into jacks-of-all-trades and masters of almost all of them. It was almost always the case that everything they owned they made themselves. They shaped their furniture out of the local trees and they made their own shoes, candles, and soap. One of their major winter activities from Kentucky to Maine was making maple sugar, and they became talented at preserving food. Usually their house was near a big spring, over which they built a spring-house where they stored butter and milk and other perishable commodities.

Growing Food

After getting suitable living quarters, the next essential activity was providing proper foods in sufficient quantities. Wild game and fowls were abundant, but these had to be supplemented by vegetables and fruit. If the Scotch-Irishman arrived in the fall or winter, his neighbors gave him enough preserved food until he could grow his own. He planted a garden in the spring close to his house so he could keep deer, foxes, rabbits, and other predators away from it.

To clear land the Scotch-Irish girdled trees, unlike the English and Germans who simply cut them down. To girdle a tree, a man cut a wide strip of bark from around it, interrupting the flow of water and nutrients, eventually killing it.[50] In the midst of these dying trees, a Scotch-Irishman planted his first crop of corn, with enough sunlight getting through the withering leaves to make the crop a success. A year after girdling them, the Scotch-Irish cut down the trees, and usually used them for firewood. This method of getting rid of trees also made it easier to remove the stumps, as the Scotch-Irish farmer went about getting "new ground" upon which to plant his crops. He broke the soil with a wooden plow: "The ground was prepared by harrowing with a triangular wood frame with downward wooden spikes, horse drawn: its shape enabled the harrow to slip past the tree stumps without breaking too often!"[51]

Generally, the Scotch-Irishman grew just enough food for his and his family's subsistence. There was one crop, however, that he always grew in excess. That crop was corn, the most highly cultivated agricultural product in the history of America.[52] The settlers used surplus corn to make whiskey, a commodity they not only partook of themselves, but also sold to keep a bit of extra money on hand.

Some Social Diversions

While the life of the frontiersman was hard and largely unromantic, it is nevertheless true that he also had some good times as he eked out his living in the wilderness. Social diversions, once the necessities of life had been seen to, were welcome events. Among the more popular, in addition to log-raisings, were flax and candy pullings, corn huskings, quilting and spelling bees, dances, tomahawk throws, and wild turkey shoots with rifles.[53] Various contests such as wrestling matches, footracing, jumping, and "gander pulling"[54] (seeing who could pick goose feathers the quickest) were also well attended events.

Weddings were, of course, joyous affairs that tended to involve not just the bride and groom but the entire community as well. Banns (public announcements of impending marriages) were announced in church, if possible, for two consecutive Sundays,[55] but the transiency and informality of the frontier gradually did away with that custom. Scotch-Irish marriages were generally for love, but there was always a practical eye out: these unions were supposed to produce many children (ten to fourteen was a common number, with usually only half surviving)[56] who would help with the farm work,[57] reflecting the old Irish adage that "One wedding makes many."[58]

A typical certificate of marriage theoretically required that both bride and groom be of "good moral character," and have obtained the consent of their parents.[59] On the wedding day large crowds gathered at the homes of both bride and groom, and they were, to be sure, in festive moods. One game was "run for the bottle," in which two men raced from the bride's to the groom's house; the first to arrive won a bottle of whiskey.[60] The winner would usually, but not always, return to the bride's house where the spirits would be consumed in a jovial atmosphere. The Scotch-Irish loved their whiskey, but they prided themselves at being able to hold their liquor. Anyone who got drunk at a social gathering was usually severely reprimanded.

After the ceremony, which was fairly dull compared to the rest of the day's events, a large wedding dinner, the expense of which was borne by the bride's father, was held.[61] Here, vast quantities of food were consumed alike by persons who had and had not attended the wedding itself. At the end of the day, younger members of the wedding party "put the bride and groom to bed." If both did not struggle "violently in protest, it was thought that an unchristian eagerness had been exhibited."[62]

Like weddings, frontier funerals were always well attended, and frequently they, too, became socializing occasions. The corpse was laid out in the bottom room if the family lived in a log cabin, and in the parlor of more elaborate abodes. Neighbors from miles around came with food, condolences, and "the glass," which circulated freely.[63] Throughout the night, neighbors sat in and around the house of the deceased, praying and reciting from the Bible. The funeral was held in the home, with the local minister in charge, and burial was either in the family plot or in a nearby cemetery.

Scotch-Irish Speech Patterns

In their long history in America, the Scotch-Irish have both loaned and borrowed words and phrases from other nationalities, and thus there developed a distinct "Scotch-Irish" dialect. In 1984, Alan Crozier published an article in *American Speech*, titled "The Scotch-Irish Influence on American English." A telling point in this article is that "the English language was transplanted to America and Ulster at the same time." Jamestown was founded in 1607 and the Ulster Plantation two years later.[64]

At the end of his article, Crozier printed a lengthy glossary of words that seem to be associated with the Scotch-Irish. They include "diamond," which means "town square"; "Driv" and "druv" as past tenses of "drive"; "nicker," a horse's whinney; and "poke" a paper sack; "till" meaning until, "wattle," a stick for driving oxen; and "you'all" and "you'ns" as plurals of "you."[65] Two other Scotch-Irish words not listed by Crozier are "fornent," meaning opposite, and "blain," to show bashfulness.[66]

Their words and their experiences in Ulster and America led to many Scotch-Irish sayings. Several related to the weather: "The evening red and the morning gray sends the traveler on his way;" and "The evening gray and the morning red brings rain upon the traveler's head" (or "the traveler had better stay in bed"). "Rainbow at night, the sailor's delight," and "Rainbow in the morning, sailors take warning" undoubtedly dated back to their trips from Ireland to the New World.

The morning hours made the Scotch-Irish think about weather: "On a foggy morning, when there are lots of cobwebs, there will be a nice day"; "Rain before seven, clear before eleven"; and "On a cloudy morning if there is a bit of blue sky big enough to patch a pair of Dutchman's breeches, the weather will fair up." One could see a change of weather shortly ahead if one observed nuthatches going up and down a tree "making their odd noises." Wind, snow, rain, and thunder, got their share of Scotch-Irish attention with expressions like: "The wind that bloweth from the east is neither good for man nor beast''; ''Snowing meal, it will snow a great deal''; ''When the rain blows in sheets, colder weather will follow''; and when thundering, ''Sounds like we might have a spell of weather.''[67]

They also developed quaint expressions to denote their feelings. A rude person could be ''as coarse as a rag carpet''; someone in pain was ''as sore as a boiled owl'' or hurting enough ''to make his toenails ache''; and a dishonest individual was ''lower than a snake's belt buckle.'' A person who did not walk very fast was ''too slow to catch a cold''; and moved ''like dead lice was falling off him.'' A noisy, loquacious person usually proved that ''a bawling cow forgets its calf the quickest'' and two people who were alike ''were both tarred from the same stick.''

A person could be as ''mad as a wet hen,'' as ''stiff as an old cow,'' and ''tough as nails.'' Young ladies were warned, ''If a girl splashes the front of her dress while washing dishes, she will marry a drunkard.'' Some religious advice was given with ''Every idle word or thought in the judgement shall be wrought'' and ''Sunday plots come to nought.''

Other expressions took a philosophical bent: ''The inheritance of a distinguished and noble name is a proud inheritance to him who lives worthily of it,'' and ''The man who has not anything to boast of but his illustrious ancestors is like a potato—the only good belonging to him is underground.''[68]

The Scotch-Irish spread their influence throughout America to such an extent that many towns and cities in the colonies were named after those in Ulster. According to author Howard Cromie, there are eighteen cities named ''Belfast'' in the United States, along with nine called ''Antrim'' and sixteen named Tyrone.[69] These are joined by twelve Milfords, and numerous townships of Antrim, Derry, Fermanagh, and Coleraine.

The Scotch-Irish put their mark on the development of the lifestyle of the American colonies and the subsequent United States. They were religiously and educationally motivated, at one and the same time dour and joyful, practical and philosophical. They never quite got over their feeling that, as

Woodrow Wilson put it, they were the "partners of Providence."[70]

ATTITUDES TOWARD WARFARE

The Scotch-Irish And The Indians

The Scotch-Irish were no strangers to conflict. Everywhere they went, either someone found them undesirable or they themselves felt obliged to push out earlier settlers. They dislocated the Irish when they first went to Ulster in the early seventeenth century. They quickly found themselves unwelcome in the 1720s when they immigrated to Boston. Later, in Pennsylvania, the Scotch-Irish ran afoul of the Indians who were already there and detested the Quakers for not doing enough to protect the frontiers. Away from Pennsylvania, in Virginia and the Carolinas, the Scotch-Irish frequently took land by force, either from Indians or from earlier white settlers who, in Scotch-Irish opinion, were not using it properly.

It was the American Indian that steadily came to be the Scotch-Irish's greatest enemy. He had land that Scotch-Irishmen wanted; they felt they could "do what God wanted" with it better than the Indians. The result was that by the late 1730s, dispossessed bands of Indians roamed many frontier areas, becoming increasingly bitter and resentful toward the white man.

John Craig spoke about Indians traveling in western Pennsylvania in groups of twenty to fifty. They were "generally civil," but when they arrived at a household, they had to be supplied with food, "or they become their own stewards and cooks sparing nothing." Roving Indians throughout the frontier also killed white men's cattle for food supplies. Sometimes entire communities built fortifications to which they would retreat whenever it was reported that unfriendly Indians were in the area.[71]

The Indian problem was one general reason why Parliament

raised no strong objections in the late 1740s and 1750s to the Scotch-Irish coming to America. When England's great competitor for the North American continent, France, allied with numerous Indian tribes against the English, Parliament even encouraged Ulstermen to immigrate. Throughout the 1750s, for example, the owners of at least a dozen ships advertised regularly in the *Belfast Newsletter* for passengers bound for America, frequently offering financial assistance to those who needed it. Dozens more regularly made the crossings without extensively advertising their services.

Colonial Wars

The first colonial war in which the Scotch-Irish played a part was King George's War, 1744–48, known in Europe as the War of Austrian Succession (which began in 1740). Most of the action occurred in New York and New England; the war ended in 1748, with England giving back Louisbourg to France without consulting the colonial forces, an action that angered local militias, fomenting ill-will between many colonists and the Mother Country.

Between 1748 and the mid 1750s, the Ohio Valley became the main arena of conflict between Scotch-Irish settlers and various Indian tribes. The French, so it was widely claimed and believed, instigated raids against English settlements. All of these raids were dreadful, but the brutalities of some even shocked the sensibilities of hardened frontiersmen.

In the early 1750s the French built a line of forts south of Lake Erie, along the Pennsylvania border. To the consternation of the colony's Scotch-Irish inhabitants, the Pennsylvania authorities, dominated by Quakers, largely ignored these French encroachments. Farther south in Virginia, however, Lieutenant Governor Robert Dinwiddie sent an expedition headed by George Washington to Fort Le Boeuf to try to convince the French to vacate this territory (which was claimed by the English), an effort that failed. In 1754, Washington returned to the wilderness in a campaign against Fort

Duquesne, only to be rebuffed by the French and their Indian allies.

A colonist wrote to the *Belfast Newsletter* in the spring of 1754 about the growing troubles between England and France in the New World. This correspondent maintained that when France first began its extensions, it leaders actually expected to be repulsed. A lack of action, especially in Pennsylvania, encouraged the French to enlarge their activities. That the writer of this letter was Scotch-Irish, there could be no doubt. "If the French are not soon drove off," the writer informed his friends in Belfast, "and forts built by the English on the Mississippi, they will have such strongholds that it will never be in our power to expel them."[72] Still not much was done, particularly by Pennsylvania authorities, to stem the tide of French expansion.

In Virginia, however, preparations were made militarily to confront the French. British General Edward Braddock took command of Virginia forces and, with Washington as his aide-de-camp, set off for Fort Duquesne.

Braddock's army was ambushed in June, 1755, and thoroughly crushed, with more than half of his men, including himself, becoming casualties. He was a stubborn, play-by-the-book English general, who would not listen to Washington and others who insisted that Indian warfare was different from traditional European ways of fighting. His dogmatism cost hundreds of good men their lives. He insisted on the usual European battle formations, with his men standing shoulder to shoulder. This tactic did not work against Indians who fired from behind trees and other cover.

A writer to the *Belfast Newsletter* described Braddock's defeat:

> Braddock was, as everyone expected, attacked from the woods by the enemy but could see nobody to fire at, and so many of his people have been sacrificed to his obstinancy. . . . Major Washington . . . begged and prayed the General . . . to let him draw off about 300 [English and colonial soldiers] in each wing to scour the woods, but Braddock refused it. . . . [The] officers

> of Old England . . . have neither skills nor courage . . . for the Indians will kill them as fast as pigeons, and they [the English] stand no chance for a defensive or offensive.[73]

Despite these negative images of the English army, colonials were still ready, even eager, to join militias against the French and Indians. "When we raise men by beat of gong," the letter writer exclaimed, "we have such force of numbers that we have to turn many of them home again."[74]

For the next several months after Braddock's defeat, as the Scotch-Irish settlers and the Indians confronted one another, the frontiers in the Ohio Valley became dreadful places. In late 1755 and early 1756, the governors of Maryland, Virginia, and South Carolina made extensive plans for military operations against the French and Indians. South Carolina offered the Cherokee Indians £3 sterling for every scalp of the enemy (primarily Shawnee) they brought in. Accordingly, some 1,600 Cherokees planned to march against the French and their Indian allies. The colonies sought the Cherokees as allies because "they are free . . . people [who] were never conquered, never relinquished their possessions, and never surrendered" to any enemy.[75] In their expedition in early 1756 against the Shawnees, the Virginians urged the 200 Cherokees accompanying them to "spare neither age nor sex" in retaliation for Shawnee barbarities of the previous summer.

Everywhere the colonial armies met the Indians, the Shawnees, and the six peoples of the Iroquois (Mohawk, Onondaga, Oneida, Seneca, Tuscarora, and Cayuga) on the field of battle, they were generally successful against them. But these successes did not comfort hundreds of backwoods settlers who were constantly at risk from roving bands of Indians, supplied by the French with guns, ammunition, and hard liquor. One settler reported that

> Our frontiers are exposed to the most Cruel and merciless Ravages, the French and Indians making Inroads among the Back Inhabitants, slaughtering the Innocent and Defenceless; numbers are already cut off; fine plantations are left desolate,

> and many Parts of this once happy and flourishing Province become a Scene of Blood; for Peace hath fled from our Borders. . . . A generous Enemy is not so dreadful, but inhuman Savages you can have no just idea of, whose very mercies are but Cruelties.[76]

In the spring of 1756, England and France formally declared war against each other. This was the only one of the great colonial wars that would begin in America and spread to Europe. In America it was known as the French and Indian war, and in Europe as the Seven Year's War. It was a war in which an entire empire hung in the balance; its outcome determined who would be the great colonial proprietor in North America. The war ended with England and the colonies as the victors.

Continued Violence

Even after the French and Indian War, much bitterness remained between the Indians and the Scotch-Irish settlers. Some white men actually wanted to infest blankets with smallpox and distribute them to Indians, while others believed hunting parties should search out Indians and kill them. Indian resentment was manifested in Ottawa Chief Pontiac's Rebellion. In 1764 he led uprisings against the frontiersmen, especially the Scotch-Irish, all through Pennsylvania and Virginia. He was ultimately defeated, but not before thousands of people had been slain. The rank hatred between the advancing forces of white settlement and the entrenched interests of the Indians produced many legacies of conflict on the North American continent.

Even after Pontiac's forces had been dispersed at the Battle of Bushy Run, in Pennsylvania, the drive of revenge was still uppermost in the minds of many Scotch-Irishmen. In the context of all the dreadful events on the frontier, rumors and conspiracy theses were so widespread that some people thought the Jesuits were behind all the Indian attacks.

One of the unhappiest events happened with the Conestoga Indians in Lancaster County, Pennsylvania. Rumor was that these Indians, though they had not taken part in the recent war and subsequent depredations, had nevertheless supplied guns and ammunition to Scotch-Irish enemies. Accordingly, a vigilante group headed by Lazarus Stewart, a Presbyterian elder,[77] stormed the jail in Lancaster County, where the Indians had been taken for safekeeping. One day they killed six of these innocent Indians; three days later they returned and slew those remaining.[78] These were the "Paxtang Boys," who were generally known as the "Paxton Boys."[79]

The colonial authorities in Pennsylvania were mortified at the work of the Paxton Boys, and some wanted to try them for murder. This attempt caused the Paxton Boys to march on the colonial capital itself, and fears were widespread that they meant to overthrow the Quaker-dominated Pennsylvania government, or at least gain additional political powers.[80] They were met by Benjamin Franklin, who used his considerable diplomatic powers to dissuade the young hotheads, and convince them to go home. Backing up Franklin, though not very obviously, was a battery of cannon to be used only in the direst of circumstances.[81] A few years later, several of these Paxton Boys were among the first to enlist in the Revolutionary army.

Not everything was morbid between the whites and the Indians during the latter 1760s, as evidenced by the following story. Two white men were deep into Penn's woods one time hunting for game. They heard someone following them, and hid behind a tree to waylay the stranger. Much to their surprise, the person was a half-starved Indian girl. They fed the girl and took her home with them. She lived with the older of her two captors and his wife, and ultimately married the younger of the two. No one ever found out where she came from, or why she had been separated from her tribe. The community took her in and for many years she was known as "Laughing Annie."[82]

But, sadly, for each "Laughing Annie" story, there were dozens that bespoke violence, cruelty, and barbarity, by both the whites and the Indians. The whites meant to have the frontier for themselves; the Indians were determined to keep it. Not until well into the revolutionary generation were these white-Indian hostilities spawned by the French and Indian War dissipated to any considerable extent.

To be sure, the Scotch-Irish were not the only people living on the frontier in the late eighteenth century. There were Germans (especially Moravians), Swedes, English, Scots, and numerous other nationalities. None of these was more astute, however, in creating conditions to support an agriculturally-based society, than the Scotch-Irish. The Scotch-Irish were definitely the most effective in controlling and then defeating the American Indians.

For many years the Pennsylvania Scotch-Irish had railed against the Quaker majorities, arguing that not enough was being done to protect the frontiers against Indian attacks. They had taken things into their own hands when it became obvious to them that they could get little relief from Philadelphia. They carried this same principle of "helping themselves" into the quarrels with the Mother Country that heated up in the period following the French and Indian War. From 1763 on, England was the major colonizing power on the North American continent. Parliament now began to impose certain restrictions on the American colonists whom it had not bothered much in the past. (One such restriction curtailed the number of Scotch-Irish who could leave Ulster for America). A great many of the colonists, including the Scotch-Irish, protested and then openly revolted against the newly created parliamentary strictures. These activities, of course, led straight into the American Revolution.

CHAPTER SEVEN

The Era of the Revolution and Constitution

With France ousted from most of North America, the Scotch-Irish saw little threat to their properties after 1763, and thus felt they did not need the protection proferred by the English Parliament. England, now the chief landlord of the continent, turned much of its attention, heretofore reserved for the French, to the Scotch-Irish. With the Scotch-Irish feeling more independent than they had at any other time in their history and the Parliament determined to control their activities through policies of land restriction (such as forbidding white settlement west of the Alleghenies), and taxation (to help pay war debts), a breach was predictable.

Scotch-Irish Resentments

New Scotch-Irish immigrants arrived by the thousands during the twelve years immediately preceding the revolution. They came because of renewed rounds of rent increases in Ulster and reports from their kinsmen in America about free or cheap land and relatively pacified Indians.

During the French and Indian War, immigration practically stopped; it started up again in the late 1760s and by the mid-1770s it had become a floodtide. At least nineteen ships advertised regularly in 1774 and early 1775 in the *Belfast Newsletter* for passengers to the New World.[1] At least as many more ships did not advertise; thus, some thirty to forty vessels were constantly crossing the Atlantic bringing people from Ulster to various American ports. Perhaps the members of Parliament were so preoccupied with the problems of the Scotch-Irish already in America that they paid scant attention to the new arrivals.

Both the Scotch-Irish who had been in America for some time and those newly arriving bore resentments against the English government. The old ones begrudged land restriction and taxation without consent and the new ones blamed Parliament for creating the conditions that forced them out of Ireland in the first place. Parliament was accused of discontinuing the old English practice of equality for all its subjects and obtaining their consent before taking an action, particularly in reference to taxation. If consent had been sought by the Parliament, things might have turned out differently, but the English authorities were high-handed and arrogant, virtually assuring Scotch-Irish, and other colonial, resistance against them.[2]

The accumulated hatreds and resentments of Ulstermen in northern Ireland and Scotch-Irish in America toward the English contributed to the development of the revolutionary movements in the colonies. Pennsylvanian Scotch-Irish "had their finest political hour" in rallying their state to independence, and they brought Delaware and New Jersey with them.[3] In the South, the Scotch-Irish came to have "no grievances" against the eastern Virginia gentry who led the revolution; the Scotch-Irish also wanted access to the restricted land west of the Appalachians, and thus their commitment to the War of Independence ultimately became "widespread, conscious, and fundamental."[4]

One high-ranking Irish official said, "The American War of Independence was lost by the English not on the battlefields of America but in the homes and farmsteads of Ulster. This explains, too, why the American War was referred to by some observers as a 'Presbyterian rebellion.' "[5]

A "Presbyterian Rebellion"?

Much was made of the Presbyterian element in the American Revolution. Horace Walpole said, "I hear that our American cousin has run away with a Presbyterian parson, and that is the end of it." George Bancroft noted that "the first voice publicly raised in America to dissolve all connection with Great Britain came, not from the Puritans of New England, nor from the Dutch of New York, nor from the cavaliers of Virginia, but from the Scotch-Irish Presbyterians."[6] King George III was reported to have said that the revolution was caused by "those pestiferous Presbyterians. They are always in unrest, and will be until they are wiped out."[7] A Hessian captain wrote during the conflict: "Call this war by whatever name you may, only call it not an American rebellion: it is nothing more or less than a Scotch-Irish Presbyterian rebellion."[8] A Tory historian, Peter Oliver, said in 1781 that the "key agitation of public opinion are the dissenting [Presbyterian] clergymen."[9] And a British officer in South Carolina asserted that "All Presbyterian Churches are 'sedition shops.' "[10] Many of these statements were Tory exaggerations, but the fact remains that Presbyterianism greatly agitated the issues that led to revolution. William Lehmann wrote, "There is overwhelming evidence that the [Scotch-Irish] were generally sympathetic to the Patriot's cause and participated strongly in their activities."[11] James T. Lemon pointed out that "their general support of the Revolution gave the Presbyterians increased social prestige."[12] And David Doyle asserted that the Presbyterian clergy made support of the Revolution "a virtual religious obligation."[13]

Declarations of Independence

Quite some time before the Revolution, many communities, villages, and towns protested, sometimes violently, and passed resolutions and declarations against the way they were treated by the colonial governments. One of the best known of these agitations was the "Regulator" movement of North Carolina, led by a group of Scotch-Irishmen. Its purpose was to reduce the arbitrary taxation and tyrannical policies of the colonial governor, William Tryon, "the wolf of Carolina." One of the chief Regulator leaders was William Butler, who had once been a deputy sheriff in Orange County. In the spring of 1771 the Regulators confronted the colonial forces at Alamance Creek in North Carolina, said by some to be the first battle of the American Revolution. The Regulators were defeated at the Battle of Alamance Creek; some of their leaders were executed, while others escaped. Among those who left North Carolina was William Butler. His brother, John, advised him not to live in Georgia or South Carolina, but to go "to the cold, wild country of Mississippi."[14]

The defeat of the Regulators was seen a few years later as a principal reason why many southern Scotch-Irish did not support the Revolution when it first started, instead becoming Tories or "tepid Patriots." According to Kerby Miller, the Tidewater planters in North Carolina "championed the people" in the Revolution, and the old Regulators would have none of it.[15] Joseph O'Grady asserted that the eastern powers in North Carolina had "denied legitimate demands of the frontier" and now led the Revolution, wanting the Scotch-Irish to fight at their side; "The numerous appeals fell on deaf ears, however."[16] Numerous Georgia Ulstermen "remained loyal out of gratitude for the free passages . . . received from a paternalistic royal government."[17] Thus, southern Scotch-Irish support for the Revolution evolved over a number of months.

Into the decade of the 1770s, however, "declarations of independence" became increasingly numerous in New England, Pennsylvania, and the South. Historian George Bancroft told of one in New Hampshire;[18] another early one was in Hanover, near Lancaster, in Pennsylvania. Hanover had first been settled by Germans, but at this time, 1774, it was dominated politically and socially by the Scotch-Irish. The Hanover Resolves, 4 June 1774, expressed sentiments on "the present critical state of affairs'' between the colonies and the Mother Country. The recent actions of Parliament (the Intolerable Acts, following the Boston Tea Party of December 1773) were "iniquitous and oppressive." The Resolves stated that it was "the bounden duty" of the inhabitants of America "to oppose every measure which tends to deprive them of their just prerogatives." They closed on the ominous note that "in the event of Great Britain attempting to enforce unjust laws upon us by strength of arms, our cause we leave to Heaven and our rifles."[19] A few days after passage of the Hanover Resolves, another Pennsylvania town, Middletown, undertook similar proceedings.

In early 1775 the citizens in at least three communities in Virginia expressed their feelings about relations with England. From Abingdon came a resolution:

> We crossed the Atlantic and explored this uncultivated wilderness, bordering on many nations of savages, and surrounded by mountains almost inaccessible to any but those very savages. . . . But soon to these remote regions the hand of unlimited and unconstitutional power hath pursued us to strip us of that liberty and property with which God, Nature, and the rights of humanity have vested us. We are ready and willing to contribute all in our power for the support of his Majesty's government, if applied to constitutionally, [but] . . . we cannot think of submitting our liberty or property to the power of a venal British Parliament, or the will of a corrupt ministry. We are deliberately and resolutely determined never to surrender [those rights] . . . to any power on earth, but at the expense of our lives.[20]

The citizens of Fincastle, Virginia, let their feelings be known on 20 January 1775:

> We by no means desire to shake off our duty or allegiance to our Lawful Sovereign, but on the contrary, shall ever glory in being the loyal subjects of a Protestant Prince . . . so long as we can enjoy the free exercise of our Religion as Protestants, and Liberties and Properties as *British* subjects. But, if no pacific measures shall be proposed or adopted by Great Britain, and

> our enemies will attempt to dragoon us out of these inestimable privileges which we are entitled to as subjects, and to reduce us to slavery, we declare that we are deliberately and resolutely determined never to surrender them to any power upon earth but at the expense of our lives.[21]

A final Virginia action came on 22 February 1775 from the freeholders of Staunton in Augusta County, where hundreds of Scotch-Irish had settled. They sent delegates to a convention in Richmond with a resolution that read: "Many of us and our forefathers left our native land and explored this once savage wilderness to enjoy the free exercise of the rights of convenience and human nature. . . . [We] will not surrender any of these rights to any body in which we have no voice."[22]

The proclamation that received the most attention was the "Mecklenburg Declaration of Independence," created in May 1775, a month after hostilities between colonial and English forces at Concord and Lexington, Massachusetts. The Mecklenburg Declaration derived from a meeting of militia companies at Charlotte Town, North Carolina, and contained language quite similar to the national Declaration of Independence that would soon follow in July 1776: "To secure unimpaired their inalienable rights, privileges, and liberties from the dominant grasp from British imposition"[23] was a phrase not too different from "endowed by their Creator with certain unalienable rights; that among these are life, liberty, and the pursuit of happiness."[24] In fact, the wording was so similar that some people argue that Benjamin Franklin was the principal author of both the Mecklenburg Declaration and the later Declaration of Independence.[25]

North Carolina Governor Josiah Martin said on 30 June 1775 that the Mecklenburg Declaration surpassed "all the horrid and treasonable publications that the inflammatory spirits of the continent have yet produced.[26] (Perhaps the governor did not know what to expect from Mecklenburg County. A decade before, in 1766, a writer had said, "The inhabitants of Mecklenburg are entire dissenters of the most rigid kind. . . . They [have] a Solemn League and Covenant teacher settled among them. . . . They are in general adverse to the Church of England. . . . and they look upon [any action] for the better establishment of the Church as oppressive as the Stamp Act").[27] Thus, the Mecklenburgers had been working toward a break with the institutions of the Mother Country for some time.[28]

The upshot of all these resolutions and memorials was that most colonies followed Virginia's lead of 15 May 1776 in instructing their delegates to the Continental Congress in Philadelphia to proclaim freedom from Great Britain. Of course, the U.S. Declaration of Independence was not a copy of previous colonial statements, but most assuredly its authors were highly influenced by the provincial outpourings. According to historian Marc Egnal, the Revolution was largely a matter of "expansionists" who wanted to settle the interior and "non-expansionists" who thought resistance against England would cause foreign powers, notably France, to become dominant on the continent. The expansionists, he wrote, were "active in encouraging popular demonstrations among the middling and lower classes of people."[29]

Individual Reflections

It was not only colonial assemblies that made their views known on the deteriorating conditions between England and the colonies. Many individuals wrote, sometimes despairingly, about the state of things. The Reverend Alexander McWhorter was an Ulsterman who had settled in North Carolina. He believed that colonial habits had degenerated, as shown by "neglect of divine worship and abuse of the gospel light." These shortcomings were manifested in "profane swearing and cursing, intemperance, and luxury." Added to these "sins," the Reverend listed uncleanliness, lasciviousness, pride, and vanity. No wonder, he believed, that God was displeased and would bring discord between the colonies and England to show his wrath: "What less could we expect than that an offended God would have made the gathering tempest to break upon us and plunge us and our Mother Country in all the awful calamities of a civil war?''[30]

Margaret Duncan of New York wrote to William Weir in Ireland that members of Parliament were not telling the truth to the residents of Great Britain about the troubles in North America. The colonies paid their full share of the expenses in the French and Indian War, she said, even to the point that Parliament ''sent us a full sum back.''[31] She explained that ''it is not the tax but the mode of taxing we dispute.''[32] Margaret regretted that the English embargo against American ships had also included Ireland. Parliament obviously thought that Ireland would otherwise have become a cover for shipping goods of war to America; the embargo ultimately ruined many businesses along the Atlantic coastline.[33]

Diarist Jonathan Moore (previously mentioned in Chapters Three and Five) spoke about the condition of the English soldiery in America on the eve of the Revolution, and to some extent believed that their weaknesses encouraged the Scotch-Irish colonists to continue their agitations. The soldiers were ''awfully wicked,'' he said, brought on, no doubt, because ''they are used by the officers in a most tyrannical manner—like creatures of another species.''[34] Of the twenty-one English regiments in America at that time, Moore said that not more than six or seven of them had chaplains. He closed this entry in his diary by asserting, ''I would rather be a sweep chimney as a soldier in America.''[35]

The Declaration of Independence

There were some 500 Scotch-Irish communities in America when the Revolution started,[36] with well over half of them in the Southern colonies. Located in each of these settlements was at least one Presbyterian Church, whose leaders in many instances initiated the offensive against the Crown. Little wonder that the Scotch-Irish were among the first to declare a state of hostilities against England.[37]

The Scotch-Irish put their fighting abilities at the service of

George Washington and the other colonial generals. Once Washington crossed the Delaware, he was in Scotch-Irish country; he became quickly enamored of them and reportedly was very pleased to have had them in his command.[38]

The Declaration of Independence, of course, is the great symbol of the American Revolution and of the United States, and the Scotch-Irish played a part in developing it. Seven of the fifty-six signers of the Declaration were Scotch-Irish, as were nine of the first thirteen governors in the newly created states.[39] The great document was first written in the hand of Charles Thomson, who had immigrated from Maghera, north Ireland. John Dunlop, a native of Strabane in Ulster, was its first printer and is sometimes credited with changing "inalienable" to "unalienable" in the text. The son of an Ulsterman, John Nixon, was the first to read the Declaration to the public.

No one was more enthusiastic about the American cause than many of the people back in Ulster. A letter writer said, "The first efforts of the people of America in support of their rights were hailed with joy and gladness in Ireland."[40] However, when copies of the Declaration arrived (it was printed in the *Belfast Newsletter* on 27 August 1776) there were some detractors. In Ballymoney, for example, a few members of the Church of England withdrew from the social club because they thought it incumbent upon them to "resist the rebels." Most citizens of the village, however, strongly supported the colonial armies, which were made up to a great extent of their own kinsmen. The women not only gave speeches on behalf of the colonial rebels, but spent much time "with their needles in making shirts and clothing for those who were fighting in the cause of liberty on the other side of the Atlantic."[41] Ballymoney was fairly typical of villages throughout Ulster.

The *Belfast Newsletter* continued its coverage of "American Affairs" after the Revolution had started. It gave a detailed account of the battles at Concord and Lexington,[42] and referred to the colonists as "the enemy." As time passed, however, the newspaper seemed to acquire a neutral stance, as it printed stories both favorable and unfavorable to the Americans. It provided readers with long excerpts from the proceedings of the Continental Congress and many of the entire orations of Samuel Adams, and well into 1776 advertised American wheat and flour, "a cargo of the very best Quality, just now landing."[43] At the same time, the newspaper also accommodated the English side. John Exshaw, for example, published a book, *Americans Against Liberty*, "an essay on the Nature and Principles of True Freedom shewing that the Design and Conduct of the Americans tend only to Tyranny and Slavery." This book was sold by James Magee at the Bible and Crown in Belfast, and was advertised heavily in the fall of 1776 in the *Belfast Newsletter*.[44]

Activities During The Revolution

It did not take long for able-bodied men to join the militia ranks and head for Washington's army. The Paxton Boys, who a few years before had massacred several Conestoga Indians, now mobilized and set out for Cambridge, Massachusetts, the last reported location of General Washington. A letter writer of August 1775, described a continental regiment: "They are remarkably stout and hardy men, many of them exceeding six feet in height. They are dressed in white frocks or rifle shirts and round hats. These men are remarkable for the accuracy of their aim, striking a mark with great certainty at two hundred yards distance."[45]

While Scotch-Irish contingents fought in most of the battles of the American Revolution, they seemed to dominate the activities in Pennsylvania and the two Carolinas. John Armstrong, a native of North Ireland and a veteran of the French and Indian War, became a brigadier general at the onset of the Revolution. Made responsible for troop deployments throughout Pennsylvania, Armstrong participated in the battles around Philadelphia. In a 1777 letter to his friend, Thomas Wharton, Armstrong described his army's situation: "The winter position of the continental army at what is called the Forge or Valley Hill, will, we hope, chiefly preserve the County of Chester . . . whilst the attempts for the defence of the Counties of Philadelphia and Bucks appears to remain chiefly or rather wholly with the militia of the State, an effort as arduous as it is laudable, and if attended with only a partial degree of success, will be all that the most sanguine person can expect."[46]

Two battles, one on the border of North and South Carolina and the other in South Carolina, featured almost exclusively Scotch-Irish regiments fighting against the British forces. The Battle of King's Mountain, fought on 7 October 1780, was essentially a confrontation between Highland Scots, most of whose descendants remained loyal to the Crown, led by Major Patrick Ferguson (who was killed), and Ulstermen, whose forebears came from Lowland Scotland. Colonels Isaac Shelby and William Campbell, both of Ulster background, helped to attain victory at King's Mountain for the revolutionaries. Some historians say that the Battle of King's Mountain was a turning point in the war in the South because it forced British General Charles Cornwallis to retreat from North Carolina.[47]

Three months later, Daniel Morgan, a native of Ballinascreen in County Derry, embarrassed the British again at the Battle of Cowpens in South Carolina. British Lieutenant Colonel Banastre Tarleton took post in a pasture the locals called Hannah's Cowpens. Through a daring strategy, Morgan and Colonel William Washington (a second cousin of George) laid waste to Tarleton's forces. In this battle, on 17 January 1781, the British suffered 270 killed and wounded, while twelve Americans were killed and sixty-two injured. Cowpens raised the morale of American troops and dashed the morale of the British; thus, it was a highly significant event in the Revolution. Author Kenneth Roberts stated that "The battle [of Cowpens] destroyed the apathy of the people of the North and awoke them to a realization of the violence of the war in the South [and] . . . to the certainty that even the best of British leaders could be overwhelmingly defeated."[48] Roberts maintained that the victory at Cowpens set in motion the events that made it possible for Cornwallis to be cornered at Yorktown several months later.

Efforts At Peace

While the war was in progress, some efforts at conciliation continued. Well known were Edmund Burke's proposal for American dominion status and Joseph Galloway's plan for "President-Generals" and "Grand Councils" to be appointed in the colonies. Emotions were too high in most instances for any constructive work to be done. The colonists would have nothing to do with either Burke's or Galloway's ideas. In fact, Galloway, the most notable "nonexpansionist in North America"[49] and a man descended from the Scotch-Irish, was later indicted for "high treason" and departed for England to live.

A highly significant event in the Revolution was the Battle of Saratoga in September 1777 in New York. This was the first major victory for the Revolutionists, and it caused the French to make an alliance with them. The French promised to stay in the war until the Americans had achieved their independence.

The French alliance was a thorn in England's side, and it set authorities to thinking about some kind of compromise to end the Revolution without sacrificing all North American holdings.

The Colonial Office in 1779 worked out a Plan of Union between Great Britain and America. It called for a national legislature in America, to deal only with American matters, along the lines already established with the Irish Parliament. This American Legislature would be considered a branch of the British Parliament.[50]

Colonial Office personnel believed the plan would be accepted, for in their opinion, many Americans were frightened by the prospect of enduring close ties with France. Republican sentiments, these people reasoned, were too widespread for Americans to continue relations with an absolute, tyrannical monarchy.

The Colonial Office made a pitch to American Presbyterians when it evoked French Catholicism as productive of "evil consequences." If the French nation were introduced among the colonists, it would "corrupt their youths and endanger their religion."[51] Someone even suggested that the English government force all the Loyalists who had come to London to return to America and act as counterweights against the rebels.[52]

As is well known, the fighting stopped in 1781, and the Treaty of Paris was signed in 1783, bringing the Revolution to an end. The significance of the Revolution for the Scotch-Irish was summed up by Kerby Miller: "In all senses of the word . . . the Revolution was a struggle to achieve and retain an 'independence,' and their victory not only added a new gloss to Ulster Presbyterians' perception of America as land of refuge and promise but also enabled Ulster-Americans . . . to justly claim the sobriquet of 'American.' "[53]

Some authors maintain that the existence of the Scotch-Irish as a distinct ethnic group in America ended with the Revolution,[54] a conclusion that is both incomplete and inaccurate. Certainly the ships from Ulster did not stop running because the Revolution had ended; on the contrary, there was another flood of immigrants over the next several years.

The Creation of Constitutions

Each of the new states created constitutions on liberal principles. Slavery was ended in many northern states, and aristocratic privileges such as primogeniture abandoned. Even freedom of religion was made a part of several of these new constitutions.

As early as 1776, Pennsylvanians wrote a new constitution and the Scotch-Irish played a major role in producing it. They became known as the "Presbyterian Party," joining the Germans and other settlers to take power away from the Pennsylvania Quakers, a triumph, one author said, of "the leather aprons over the scions of wealth and culture."[55] However, John Ralston and John Grier, two Scotch-Irish delegates, refused to sign the 1776 Pennsylvania document because God was not mentioned in it. Moreover, Grier could not get a leave of absence from the convention to go home twenty miles away to gather buckwheat.[56]

The Pennsylvania Constitution of 1776 "reflected the democratic thought of the period."[57] All freemen twenty-one years old and older who had lived in Pennsylvania for at least a year and who could prove full payment of taxes gained the franchise.[58] Office holders had to take two oaths: first, not to do anything prejudicial to the new Constitution, and second, to express belief in one God (though as Ralston and Grier had discovered, God was not mentioned in the document itself) and divinity of the Bible.[59]

The Pennsylvania Constitution of 1780 has been called "the most radical Constitution in America."[60] It had a weak executive, and no upper house at all. It was created by a combination of "Ulster frontier elements" and radicals in the eastern part of the state.[61]

The Scotch-Irish did not dominate or even take the lead at the creation of all these new state constitutions. Their ideas, however, were put forward to delegations with such intensity that frequently they were adopted as a part of the new systems. The Scotch-Irish, while plentiful in all of the thirteen original states, had no numerical domination in any of them. Thus, they never developed rigid ties to any particular colony, as the Puritans did in Massachusetts.[62] This caused them to be less states' rightists, in some instances at least, than their constitutional brethren, and more amenable to a centralized form of government. They certainly did not, however, lose any of their love of independence, self-reliance, or general distrust of outsiders. These characteristics were practiced in the framework of the different occupations Scotch-Irishmen pursued. Generally, the more industrialized and mercantilistic the Scotch-Irish became in various parts of the country, such as the Middle Atlantic states, the more inclined they were to accept the idea of governmental centralization. The more agriculturally oriented they became such as in the South and large portions of New England, the more provincialist and states' rights sentiments tended to prevail.[63]

During the period 1781–87 Americans chafed under the

restraints of the Confederacy. Many Scotch-Irish became businessmen once they got to America, and they found that the Articles of Confederation made it difficult, if not sometimes impossible, to conduct business on an interstate basis. The Scotch-Irish also became active in land speculation after the Revolution; again, they found, just as George Washington did, that having to comply with the rules and regulations of thirteen different governments instead of just one centralized authority was cumbersome, wasteful of time and profit, and quite nettlesome. They applauded Washington's efforts to make things easier for the entrepreneurs and speculators in America. The Scotch-Irish, therefore, generally supported the federal Constitution that was completed in September, 1787. The first state to accept the new Constitution was Delaware, which had always had a large contingent of Scotch-Irish settlers. New Jersey and Pennsylvania, other areas of heavy Scotch-Irish population, also quickly accepted the federal Constitution. Most of the states ratified the Constitution in 1788, while others—and this included agriculturally dominated, Scotch-Irish-influenced North Carolina—waited until 1789 and beyond. The latter based their objections on arguments about states' rights and the loss of independence under the new Constitution.

Did the Scotch-Irish strongly influence the ideas that were put into the federal Constitution? Some authors say no.[64] They had shown for years in their religious organization, however, that they liked hierarchical arrangements in which decisions could be appealed to higher authorities. Their organization of church, presbytery, synod, and general assembly was not too unlike the federalism of local, state, and national levels of government that emanated from the Constitution. Likewise, the Scotch-Irish, in their lengthy history both in Ireland and America, had come to believe that governmental authority had to be shared; thus, they favored the checks and balances among the legislative, executive, and judicial departments of the federal government provided by the Constitution of 1787, with probably a slight bias for a bicameral congress. Like most Americans of the day, the Scotch-Irish distrusted executive power (in their opinion, George III was nothing if not a typical administrator), and so they favored legislative power over the executive. For the first forty years of the Republic, presidents were regarded more in the "moderator" or "temperate" sense of good Presbyterianism than in the "all-powerful" connotations of Chief Executive. Ironically, it was the seventh president, Andrew Jackson, whose parents had come from Carrickfergus in County Antrim, who brought the first real power and authority to the American presidency.

Conclusions

It had been almost two hundred years since the Lowland Scots settled in northern Ireland at the behest of King James I of England. During those two centuries the Scotch-Irish faced one obstacle, both man-made and natural, after another. Always influencing the events of the day, but never dominating, the Scotch-Irish helped to clear the frontiers for westward movements of white settlers. They were indispensable to the British against the French, only to turn their long pent-up wrath against the Mother Country itself in the Revolution. The same generation that fought the American Revolution also wrote the federal Constitution of 1787. In terms of its contributions to American posterity, it was a remarkable generation.

The revolutionary era marked the end of the old immigration from Ulster to North America. These were the immigrants who had come in search of land upon which to support themselves and families. To them, little was more important than ownership, not leasing, of land. They tended to dislike crowded cities and embraced the isolation, even loneliness, of the frontier regions. They were standoffish, generally keeping to themselves. Besides acquisition of land, the Scotch-Irishmen came to America for religious freedom. Many of the characteristics with which Americans have been identified through the years (pragmatism, love of success, reform impulses) they acquired in part from these pioneering Scotch-Irish immigrants.

The new Scotch-Irish were, like the old, the products of unhappy times in their British homeland. Though they were highly inured to an agricultural way of life, they settled more in the cities than their old antecedents. They took a part in the rapidly developing industrial centers of the country during the closing years of the eighteenth and the opening years of the nineteenth centuries. The new seemed also to differ from the old in matters of religion and society. They were not quite as pious as their forebears, joining many times in enlightened views of the day. Though there were differences, the new immigrants from Ulster were just as Scotch-Irish as the old ones had been. From 1783 to 1813, approximately 100,000 immigrants came from Ulster to the United States.[65]

CHAPTER EIGHT

Post Revolutionary Immigrations

The "New" Scotch-Irish

During the American Revolution, the number of English troops on duty in Ireland dwindled to a low of 3,000, a condition that led to numerous unpleasant events. France and Spain attempted new inroads into the island, necessitating the mobilization of 80,000 militiamen to fend them off. Without the British army to prevent it, the Catholics and Protestants literally waged war on each other. One letter writer believed that England deliberately kept protective forces away from Ireland: "The ruling powers [have] long artfully fomented religious prejudices between the two great bodies of which the people were principally composed, . . . with the Presbyterians of the North and Roman Catholics of the South, who they merely made instruments for mutually enslaving each other."[1]

Besides war and growing religious problems, Ulstermen found many economic motives for continued immigration to the United States. During the British conflict with America and France, much of Irish produce was forced to go to the war effort. Commodities again became scarce and, accordingly, their prices shot up. Within a month after the Treaty of Paris in 1783, ships once more headed from Ulster to America with hundreds of north Irish immigrants aboard. Before the end of the year some 5,000 persons had sailed for the New World.[2] In 1784, Ulster immigration to America exceeded 10,000 people.[3] Between the end of the Revolution and the beginning of the War of 1812, some 150,000 Ulstermen made their way to the United States. These groups included not only the "respectable" classes made up of farmers and artisans, but also thousands of indigent persons, which ultimately caused concern among various municipal authorities. A vessel from Newry landed in 1796 in New York with approximately 300 destitute passengers. The city government used their arrival to launch a campaign for the state rather than the city to care for these people.[4]

The new Scotch-Irish differed in many ways from the old, but Scotch-Irish they nevertheless were. They were not frontier-minded, because they tended to join friends and relatives in already established communities throughout Pennsylvania, Virginia, and North Carolina. Too, they moved in great numbers into large eastern seaboard cities like Philadelphia, Baltimore, and New York.[5] Even if they left the east, they found, as one author said, more "mobility and wider opportunity of life" in nineteenth century America than their earlier counterparts. Thus, compact settlements of the Scotch-Irish did not exist as much as previously, making it possible for the New Scotch-Irish immigrants ultimately to be absorbed into an American society.[6]

The new Scotch-Irish did not relate as much as the old to agricultural pursuits, opening of frontiers, and confronting the Indians. Rather, they joined an America that was becoming increasingly industrialized and urbanized. They were not as committed as their old counterparts to Presbyterianism, showing a comparatively liberal proclivity, not only in religion, but in politics and economics as well. These urban Scotch-Irish became Jeffersonian, expressing hatred toward the Federalists, whom they equated with the ruling Tory factions in England. In the early 1790s, when American public opinion was sharply divided over the French-English war that emanated from the

French Revolution, the new Scotch-Irish were definitely pro-French and anti-English.

Also, the new Scotch-Irish did not support the recently created United States Constitution as much as their elder brethren. The old Scotch-Irish had played a role in creating the document and had become fairly centrist in the post revolutionary period. The new Scotch-Irish, coming from an environment of religious and economic oppression, quite frequently experienced many freedoms (religion, speech, expansion) for the first time in their lives. They became states' rightists in philosophy, wanting organized government to keep its distance.

Taxes

Between 1792 and 1794 the first major problem occurred between the United States government and the Scotch-Irish: the Whiskey Rebellion in western Pennsylvania. For years, farmers in the Pittsburgh area, most of whom were Scotch-Irish, had turned their surplus corn into whiskey. With 570 distilleries (one to every six or seven farmers)[7] they produced not only for personal consumption, but also for sale, without paying any local or federal taxes. David Doyle said of the rebellion: "The stills themselves were treated as a form of capital, the whiskey as currency (besides its massive straight consumption). As in Ulster, whiskey as diversion and as money-substitute over-lapped; as in both Ireland and Scotland, excise was regarded as tyrannical intervention by government into the realm of hearth and trade."[8]

Secretary of the Treasury Alexander Hamilton, himself descended from the Scotch-Irish on his mother's side, treated the Pennsylvania corn farmers as a test case with respect to the federal government's ability not merely to lay taxes, but to collect them as well. (It may be recalled that under the Confederacy, the national government had difficulty collecting taxes that had been levied and that the old Scotch-Irish came to dislike the weaknesses of the Articles of Confederation). He recommended that President Washington send troops into southwestern Pennsylvania to put down the rebellion. Washington accommodated Hamilton, but not before the rebels came close to burning Pittsburgh itself. They were largely dissuaded from this drastic action by Presbyterian clergy in the area. The Whiskey Rebellion was an outbreak of states' rights sentiments in opposition to the power of a centralized U.S. government.

Another revenue that the Scotch-Irish, both old and new, objected to paying was the glass tax, imposed in the 1790s by several American states. The glass tax, a revenue that had also been levied in the Old Country, was imposed according to the number of panes in dwelling-house windows, causing many builders to construct completely windowless abodes.[9] As a result, in many instances, log residences were plastered on the inside with mud and lime, and then whitewashed to improve interior visibility.

Despite their objections to taxes of various kinds, the Scotch-Irish by the 1780s were not poor. Even back in Ulster, they had been reluctant to display their prosperity, "lest it invite the rapacity of laird, landlord, merchant, or tithe proctor."[10] By 1782, Scotch-Irish representation among the top taxpayers in Chester and Lancaster Counties in Pennsylvania "was the same as their share of the whole population."[11] Thus, it was not based as much on their inability to pay the taxes imposed upon them as it was on their general feeling toward governmental powers.

Reasons for New Immigration

By far the greatest reasons for the immigration of the new Scotch-Irish in the 1790s was the deplorable state of affairs in Ulster between opposing religious groups. In 1792 the United Irishmen formed to "cultivate a brotherhood of affection with Irishmen of every religious persuasion," which would "endeavor to procure a fair and equal representation of all the people of Ireland."[12] Its leaders, Wolfe Tone and Lord Edward

Fitzgerald, were much more radically minded than Henry Grattan, the Protestant leader who had worked for Irish reform throughout the 1780s. Among other things, Tone and Fitzgerald wanted to unite the Catholics of the South with the Presbyterians of the North, for a concerted opposition to England's rule. At one time, an estimated 600,000 people belonged to the United Irishmen, each of whom paid a pence a week membership dues.

Though their early propounders argued that they were primarily political, the United Irishmen were quickly labeled as religious activists, a supposition that worried British authorities. Government spies infiltrated the United Societies and people identified as members were arrested and thrown into prison, with their homes and property frequently destroyed.[13]

In addition to sending in the army to control the United Irishmen (who became identified with Roman Catholicism), the British government also encouraged the formation of the Orangemen to act as a counterpoise. Trouble began almost immediately between these two groups, creating conditions in the years ahead that often reached despicable proportions.

The deteriorating conditions in Ireland may be perceived through letters from James Steele to his brother Ephraim, who, about 1790, settled in Philadelphia. On 5 March 1791 James reported from Belfast that "there is a growing rebellion hear," in part because of the English parliament's increasingly militant stance against *all* of Ireland, and because of a "great dearth of victuals," brought on by a "late wet harvest." The country, James said, was "full of poor people going begging."[14] During the next five years things did not improve. In April 1796, James told Ephraim that "their is every appearance of troublous times here," with "operations . . . greater and greater every day." There were such increases in taxes (including special ones to finance the incessant wars between England and France), duties on groceries, and enforcement of tithes that no one could say "what he has is his own." Thus, James claimed, there was a "great deal of insurrection" in Ireland. It was as though the doleful conditions of the 1640s were being reenacted.

By the following year, 1797, war had again broken out with the French. James wrote to Ephraim that the English government thought Ireland "wished for the French to come in here. Our magistrate thinks that the country [Ireland] is united by oath against [England], but I will not give you any thought of it."[15] In this and other letters, James mentioned the Orangemen, "sworn to be true to King George & to destroy all Romans."[16]

One of the worst aspects of the renewed religious and political problems in Ireland was that people could be accused and punished by innuendo and association rather than hard evidence. Such was the case of the Caldwell family in Balleymoney. Because Richard Caldwell became a general in the army of the United Irishmen, his father's house was burned to the ground, even though the father knew nothing of his son's participation.[17] The British major who with his men carried out the order gave the Caldwell's five minutes to get their belongings out of the house before it was torched. The family lived for several days after the event under a carpet thrown over two hedges. Richard was later arrested in Scotland, brought back to Coleraine, court-martialed, and given a sentence of death. The authorities in London, however, did not confirm the court-martial's finding, and Richard's sentence was commuted to exile in the United States.[18] Even so, General George Nugent detained Richard until his father signed an affidavit swearing that *each and every one* of the Caldwell family would sail for America. Throughout the summer of 1798 members of the family departed at various times, and in August they were all reunited in Salisbury Mills, New York, where they went into the linen and wholesale grocery business.

Rebellion of '98

In 1798 uprisings occurred throughout Ireland, which all but left the country in a state of ruin. The Rebellion of '98, often called the Wolfe Tone Revolt, came about because of the continuing clashes between Orangemen and United Irishmen, and the English government's attempt to put down the latter. In the renewal of war with France, English authorities had learned of United Irish correspondence with French Republican officials, who had promised to aid their cause. Now, in addition to inciting religious and political uprisings, the United Irish were accused of treason against the crown.

General Gerard Lake's English forces met the United Irish rebels at Vinegar Hill in County Wexford and put them down most cruelly, in retaliation for an earlier action when the rebels had piked several royalists and thrown their bodies into the river.[19] In other instances, rebel groups, sometimes led by priests, were smashed by the English army and its Irish Protestant collaborators. Adding to these turmoils was the arrival, in spring 1798, of a small French force of 1,000 men at Killala Bay. It, too, was quickly repulsed.

Reports throughout the spring of 1798 told of robberies and murders all over the country, with the army kept busy confiscating arms belonging to the United Irishmen. James Moore of Moneyrabane was wanted for the slaying of Pat Finlay. When Moore was caught, he was on the verge of embarking for America.[20] William Magill was hanged on a lamppost opposite Market House in Belfast. Cleland Colvin, a carpenter from Newtownards, was sentenced to 800 lashes of the whip for "seditious practices." The *Belfast Newsletter* reported that he took 600 of them at one session, but gave no description of his condition afterward.[21] A woman's head was shaved for giving false information to the authorities. Rewards were offered for several persons charged with "high treason," including Richard McCormack, Edward Rattigan, and William Lawless, most of whose families fled the country because of its troubles and immigrated to America. All things considered, 1798 and 1799 were among the worst years in Ireland's history. Antrim, Ballymore, Balleyclose, Templepatrick, Killead, Doagh, Randalstown, and Balleymoney, suffered the most by "fire and sword."

A letter writer during the rebellion asserted that "nothing remains . . . but the ruins of burnt towns and houses in the country. . . . In Coleraine four or five men were hanged upon one day."[22] Another writer said that "people go out into the forest and live unprotected like beasts,"[23] and that Britain's business of "imprisoning, ravishing, hanging, and burning" was done "with the actual determination to blot out the name of United Irishmen from under heaven."[24]

As the rebels were gathered up and brought to trial, there were three major types of punishment handed out. The one most used, at least for the leaders, was execution; another was seven to fourteen years in His Majesty's service somewhere in the world; finally, there was exile to the United States. Wolfe Tone, a leader in the rebellion, was court-martialed in November 1798 and sentenced to death, but he committed suicide in prison. Thomas Townsley of Balloo was found guilty of treason and "transported for life" to America. Thomas Burch was given a choice of service to the king, or "banishment" to America. John Orr, in a Belfast prison, "feared" that he would "be obliged to go to America."[25] Even those who were let off by the British still had to take the following loyalty oath to the crown: "I do solemnly promise and swear that I will bear true allegiance to His Majesty King George the Third, his heirs and successors, and I do hereby renounce and abjure all oaths and engagements of every kind, whatsoever, which are in any degree contrary thereto. So help me God."

Letters between America and Ireland spoke frequently of the troubles. "Young men of the best fortunes plan to leave here [Ulster] for America," said one correspondent.[26] "What remains for poor Ireland?" asked another; "nothing is now even to be hoped for."[27] It became a common practice for relatives and friends on both sides of the Atlantic to begin their letters to each other with "Dear ______________ if yet alive."

On into the new century, as England and Napoleonic France fought each other, the Scotch-Irish in the United States continued to urge their kinsmen back in Ireland to immigrate. Some were advised not even to think about what profession they might follow once they got to America. "I really think it imprudent to determine on any particular business prior to your leaving Ireland," said one letter writer, "for there might be opportunities after your arrival of getting into a very different one that would be more to your advantage."[28] Echoing this sentiment, another person remarked that "The United States do undoubtedly promise much to emigrants of every description, provided they are industrious and well conducted, but no country under Heaven throws more obstacles in the way of any idle or dissolute man procuring a livelihood."[29]

Return of the Tories

Contrary to the belief in Ulster, however, that after some time in America the Scotch-Irish became hard-hearted toward their friends and relatives still in the Old Country, letters back home sometimes spoke of shedding tears over the conditions that prevailed throughout Ireland. Apparently, some Scotch-Irishmen had contemplated a return visit to Ulster, but in 1807 the Tories came to full power (after a year of a coalition government following the death of Pitt the Younger in early 1806) under the leadership of the Duke of Portland. The Tories were anathema to the Scotch-Irish, both those still living in Ulster and those who had gone to the United States. Under Pitt the Younger's leadership, the Whigs had fairly well controlled the more precipitous actions of George III, turning him in effect, into a constitutional monarch. Ulstermen everywhere had lived improved lives during the second ministry of Pitt the Younger, from 1803 to 1806.

The return of the Tories, however, çaused Ulstermen to want to immigrate, and changed the minds of many immigrants about coming back to the Old Country. A letter writer expressed his opinion that "the change of administration which has lately taken place in England has cooled the wishes of many for seeing once more their native soil."[30] The change, he went on, promised "good neither for this country [the United States] or any other country."[31] The friends of "general liberty" had been struck a blow by Tory resurgence.

The Ulster immigration continued to America in great numbers from 1807 to 1812; perhaps as many as 50,000 people made their way from north Ireland to various parts of the

United States, and, importantly, many of these were professional men (physicians, lawyers, and craftsmen).[32] The immigration of this five year period before the War of 1812 affected the friends of reform in Ireland itself because some of the best citizens were leaving the country, the very citizens upon whom many had depended to resist Tory and monarchical encroachments.

It was more the War of 1812 than the American Revolution that slowed, at least for a time, the general flow of Ulstermen to North America. After the conflict, immigration did not immediately resume its previous levels because, in large part, the Tories under the Liverpool ministry (1812–1827) were preoccupied with large spread discontent in England itself. The English Parliament passed laws (an income tax, the Corn Laws, and the Six Acts, among others) that were despised by most of the English populace. The severity of these acts created unsettled conditions leading to riots in 1817 and the Peterloo Massacre in 1819, and ultimately produced far-reaching reforms under the ministry of Charles, Earl Grey, in 1832. The Parliament had been much affected by the outbreak of yet another revolution in France in 1830. It seemed that revolution in France usually caused reform in England.

The upshot of these events in England from 1812 to 1832 was that Ulstermen generally benefitted; a saying arose that "England's difficulty is Ireland's opportunity." Not the least of Ireland's gain during the period was a modicum of free trade; for the first time in history, under Board of Trade President William Huskisson, foreign countries in 1823 could trade directly with British colonies, a situation that helped the economic condition of Ulster.

Letters from Immigrants

Letters from the immigrants continued to flow into Belfast and other parts of Ulster, urging their countrymen to join them in the United States. Robert Given of "Mobile Alabama State; West Florida," told his father that ten pence in Ireland was thought of as a dollar in America. He spoke of "inhabitants of this country" accumulating property and then not working at all, instead letting their cattle roam wild in the woods.[33] In America, said another letter writer, one could always get the "right connections" if he knew someone of "good property."[34]

John Anderson of Vianna, Ohio, wrote to his parents in Ballinrees, Londonderry, that "no doubt your clay house is muldring. . . . and your heads getting gray and wrinkles in your brow," and then he strongly urged his brother to immigrate to America:

> I like this country well and I think [you] could do better than in Ireland. Common victuals here are white bread, potatoes, pork, butter, cheese, pie, applesauce, cake, coffey, tea. . . . Land is £8 an acre. . . . You had a pretty hard time in Ireland last winter for the want of turf. We are not at a loss for a fire here. With two men and a yoke of oxen you could get as much wood in four days as in a year at Ballinrees.

John told his brother to bring his own bride from home, for he thought "the girls here are not as hansome as in Ireland." He claimed that some of the young Scotch-Irish immigrants in his area were saving money for passage home to get wives and then return to the United States.[35] In reference to wives, James Weir of Belfast asked his niece in Philadelphia to inform young men of her acquaintance that if they did not come home, the young ladies they knew in Ireland "will have ceased to be such, and you will lament your delay."[36]

Another letter writer unknowingly spoke prophetically when he told a relative, "We don't plant as many potatoes here as you do in the old country, but we can rase more on the same quantity of ground."[37] It was the potato, more than anything else, that caused Irish immigration, both north and south, to resume in the late 1840s. Black rot ruined the potato crops of 1846 and those of the next two years. The result was that lands were abandoned, mass starvation occurred, and immigrants to America from over the entire country, not just Ulster, came by the hundreds of thousands—more than twice as many as had come before the Revolution. The great Irish immigration of 1849 caused by the potato famine led, according to some scholars, to the name "Scotch-Irish" itself. It was said that Ulster Presbyterians began calling themselves "Scotch-Irish" to distinguish themselves from their Catholic counterparts. (See Chapter One, however, for other explanations of how the term arose). The immigration of the Irish in general caused the older groups of Scotch-Irish to be merged as "Irish" more than ever before, at least in the minds of most Americans. In this sense, it may be said that the Scotch-Irish as a distinct group probably ended sometime between 1800 and 1850.

Scotch-Irish Significance

The Scotch-Irish in America are best remembered historically as frontier people and military men. In a sense, they were loners, going places where few others were interested. They dealt with the possible, getting as much from it as they could. They produced more generals, politicians, and newspapermen than poets, artists, and writers.

Among the military people and politicians, Andrew Jackson and U. S. Grant stand out. Jackson was first generation Scotch-Irish. His father, Andrew, Sr., and his mother, Elizabeth (Hutchinson) came from Boneybefore, Carrickfergus, in County Antrim. In 1765 Andrew, Sr., became "discontented with the humdrum life of an Ulster farmer", and sailed for America. They settled in the Waxhaw area of South Carolina, and five days before Andrew, Jr., was born, his father died.[38] Ulysses S. Grant was Scotch-Irish on his mother's side. In 1879, after his presidency, he made a much celebrated tour of north Ireland, where he generally made a fool of himself. He remarked as he gazed over the Ulster countryside: "I don't see why they didn't all emigrate."[39] One of his aides, General Adam Badeau, asserted that General Grant had "presided over more Ulstermen than Queen Victoria," which was a true, but not very diplomatic statement.[40] Other presidents who claimed

Scotch-Irish descent either through one or both parents included John Adams, James Monroe, James K. Polk, James Buchanan, Andrew Johnson, Grover Cleveland, William McKinley, Chester Arthur, Benjamin Harrison, Theodore Roosevelt, Woodrow Wilson, Harry Truman, Dwight Eisenhower, and Richard Nixon. Howard Cromie pointed out that in the ninety-two years "from the start of . . . Jackson's presidency to the end of . . . Wilson's, the White House was occupied for fifty-six of those years by men of Scotch-Irish descent."[41] Another author estimated that four percent of Great Britain's population had fathered thirty percent of U.S. presidents.[42]

Among the Scotch-Irish who became prominent as newspapermen were Horace Greeley of the New York *Tribune*, Joseph Medill of the *Chicago Tribune*, and Robert Bonner of the *New York Ledger*. Inventors included Robert Fulton, Samuel F. Morse, and Cyrus McCormack. Prominent writers like Mark Twain, Edgar Allan Poe, and F. Scott Fitzgerald claimed Scotch-Irish ancestry.

The vast majority of the Scotch-Irish in America were like most other immigrant groups: common, ordinary, hard-working people trying to make a livelihood for themselves and their families. They were no more heroic than other immigrants; they simply played their part in settling the North American continent. Some of the distinctly "American" characteristics that the Scotch-Irish have helped to contribute are pragmatism, a reliance on "workability" factors; individualism, sometimes to such an extent that they became the prototype for the well-known "loner" in U.S. history; and self reliance, which caused them not to want too much governmental assistance on the one hand or regulation on the other. Not the least of the accomplishments of the Scotch-Irish were the songs they wrote and played. Their music was a mixture of Old World remembrances and New World experiences, with many of their songs ending with C sharp, suggesting a sequel. According to one author, the Scotch-Irish "invented" what we know today as "country music,"[43] with its usual themes of barroom brawls and lost love. Also, the Scotch-Irish moved around a great deal, and perhaps this movability explains, in part at least, the historic mobility of the American people.

Resurgence of Scotch-Irish History

For many years after the Scotch-Irish ceased to be a distinct group in America, few, if any, studies were made of their history and significance to the American experience. One person asserted that the "Scotch-Irish were too busy making history to write any of it."

The first Scotch-Irish Congress met on 8 May 1889 in Columbia, Tennessee. Out of this meeting of people interested in the Scotch-Irish, the Scotch-Irish Society of the United States was formed later in the year. Its principal founders were A. K. McClure and J. S. MacIntosh, both Pennsylvanians. The objectives of the society were fourfold: historical, educational, fraternal, and patriotic. It wanted to preserve Scotch-Irish history, and keep alive the "esprit de corps of the race," and promote "social intercourse and fraternal feeling among its members now and hereafter." It tried, largely unsuccessfully, to encourage "the younger generation" to study the Scotch-Irish.

The Scotch-Irish Society organized congresses during the 1890s and on into the 1900s. These annual meetings brought together both scholar and laymen with abiding interests in the Scotch-Irish. Beyond socializing, several learned papers were presented at these sessions. State societies sprang up, following the national model, in California, Pennsylvania, Tennessee, Virginia, North Carolina, Georgia, Kentucky, and Iowa.

By 1949 only one of these state societies survived, that of Pennsylvania. One person lamented that not only had the Scotch-Irish "vanished from the scene of American life. . . . They have left no trace of their existence, save a few volumes of speeches and articles." There was no single library or institute devoted to gathering Scotch-Irish materials. Accordingly, the Scotch-Irish Foundation was formed in 1949, not simply to have annual meetings and learned seminars, but to "search for, acquire, hold, store and preserve" books, documents, and historical materials of every kind and description, "relating to the origin and history of the Scotch-Irish people in Scotland, Ireland, and the United States."[44] Genealogy was high on the list of priorities of the Scotch-Irish Foundation. The Balch Institute for Ethnic Studies in Philadelphia became the chief repository of all materials gathered by the Scotch-Irish Foundation. In addition to the Foundation, Scotch-Irish history has been kept alive through the heritage festivals that are held each year. They are composed of scholars and laymen alike, and alternate their meetings between the United States and Ulster. Papers presented at these festivals range from how the term "Scotch-Irish" originated to descriptions of their activities once they reached North America.

Conclusions

It has been said, with some exaggeration, that the Scotch-Irish were the most "American" of all the immigrant groups who came to British North America. They were a group that ultimately backfired considerably against the British Parliament. No efforts were made to stop them from leaving Ireland; in fact, while Britain fought the French, the Scotch-Irish were actually *encouraged* to travel. The Scotch-Irish subsequently became one of England's greatest enemies on the eve of the American Revolution. The Revolution stopped Scotch-Irish immigration, at least for a time. During the post-revolutionary period, from 1783 to 1812, immigration resumed, numbering into the tens of thousands. There were differences between the pre-and-post revolutionary Scotch-Irish immigrants, but they were both Scotch-Irish, and they both came to North America for essentially the same reasons. From 1812 to 1850, especially during the potato famine, Scotch-Irish immigration was so intertwined with south Irish arrivals that little distinction was made between the two. Thus, "Scotch-Irish" and "Irish" became as one in the general American mind. It was during the first fifty years of the nineteenth century that the Scotch-

Irish became generally assimilated into the mainstream of American life.

Today, some 22 million Americans claim Scotch-Irish ancestry. There are no distinct communities of Scotch-Irish today. They are scattered throughout the length and breadth of the United States. Though they claim no distinctive areas of settlement, it is nevertheless true that almost every American of Scotch-Irish descent knows of his heritage, and is proud of it. The Scotch-Irish were right at the heart of the American experience, and, in more ways than one, they have remained so, even into our own time.

Notes

FOREWORD

1. Bernard Bailyn, *Voyagers To The West: A Passage In the Peopling of America On the Eve of the Revolution* (New York: Random House, 1986), 25.

2. Winthrop D. Jordon, *White Over Black: American Attitudes Toward The Negro, 1550–1812* (Chapel Hill, N.C.: University of North Carolina Press, 1968), 339.

3. Louis B. Wright, *The Cultural Life of the American Colonies, 1607–1763* (New York: Harper & Bros. 1957), 46.

4. David Noel Doyle, *Ireland, Irishmen and Revolutionary America, 1760–1820*. (Dublin and Cork: The Mercier Press, 1981), 51–52.

5. Bernard Bailyn, *The Peopling of British North America: An Introduction* (New York: Random House, 1985), 36.

6. Jordon, *White Over Black*, 103.

7. For further discussions on this question, see William Forbes Adams, *Ireland, and Irish Emigration to the New World From 1815 to the Famine* (New Haven, Conn.: Yale University Press, 1932).

8. Terry Coleman, *Going To America* (New York: Pantheon Books, 1972), i.

CHAPTER ONE

1. Wallace Notestein, *The Scots in History* (New Haven: Yale University Press, 1946; reprinted by Greenwood Press, 1970), 9.

2. Ibid.

3. Ian Finlay, *Scotland* (Oxford: Oxford University Press, 1944), 4.

4. Ibid.

5. M. Perceval-Maxwell, *The Scottish Migration to Ulster In The Reign Of James I* (London: Routledge & Kegan Paul, 1973), 22.

6. The story of how Ayr was named goes this way: Once in battle, a fully armored Scots king was thrown from his horse. The force of the fall caused his armor to bend around his neck, so that he was in danger of suffocation.

A young soldier, seeing the plight of his king, jumped from his horse and ran, among flurries of arrows, to him. The soldier freed the king from the bent armor, and the monarch began breathing again.

While freeing the king, the young soldier had been hit by a sword, which ultimately cost him a leg.

After the battle, the king knighted the young soldier. The king stated, "For risking your life and freeing the armor-plate round my neck—give me air to breathe—I knight you 'Sir Ayr.' "

Today, the coat of arms for the Scots-descended Ayr and Ayer families shows a leg on a shield of armor, commemorating the time their ancestor saved a king's life. Samuel C. Ayer of New Castle, Delaware, letter to the author, 2 March 1987.

7. Henry Grey Graham, *Social Life of Scotland in the 18th Century* (New York: Benjamin Bloom, 1971), 5.

8. Finlay, *Scotland*, 25.

9. Perceval-Maxwell, *The Scottish Migration*, 41.

10. Ibid. James G. Leyburn, *The Scotch-Irish: A Social History* (Chapel Hill, N.C.: University of North Carolina Press, 1962), 16–17.

11. Notestein, *The Scot in History*, 96.

12. Finlay, *Scotland*, 18.

13. As an illustration, a popular story in America about Scot stinginess went this way: A man died, and three friends came to see him lying in state. The Englishman put $15.00 in his friend's casket to help pay expenses on the long road to heaven. The Frenchman contributed another $15.00. The Scotsman walked up to the casket, wrote a check for $45.00, collected the $30.00 in cash in change, and walked away.

14. From Sir Anthony Weldon, quoted in P. Hume Brown ed., *Early Travelers in Scotland* (New York: Burt Franklin, 1891), 97.

15. Maury Klein, "The Scotch-Irish: A Race In Upheaval," *American History Illustrated* 13: 9, (January, 1979): 31.

16. Brown, *Early Travelers in Scotland*, 98.

17. Leyburn, *The Scotch-Irish*, 33.
18. Brown, *Early Travelers in Scotland*, 14.
19. Graham, *Social Life of Scotland*, 8–10.
20. Ibid., 12.
21. Finlay, *Scotland*, 13.
22. Graham, *Social Life of Scotland*, 14.
23. Ibid., 8–10. Also, Leyburn, *The Scotch-Irish*, 16–17.
24. Leyburn, *The Scotch-Irish*, 16–17.
25. Ibid., 48.
26. Klein, "The Scotch-Irish", 30–36.
27. Ibid.
28. Leyburn, *The Scotch-Irish*, 73; Finlay, *Scotland*, 6.
29. Finlay, *Scotland*, 15.
30. Perceval-Maxwell, *The Scottish Migration*, 255.
31. Thomas F. Hudson, "The Source of the Term Scotch-Irish," in *Selected Proceedings of Scotch-Irish Heritage, Festival II at Winthrop College, November 17–19, 1983*. (Baton Rouge, La.: VAAPR, 1984).
32. Klein, "The Scotch-Irish" A Race in Upheaval," 30–36.
33. William V. Shannon, *The American Irish* (New York: MacMillan, 1963), viii–ix.
34. Carl Frederick Wittke, *We Who Built America: The Saga of the Immigrant* (New York: Prentice-Hall, 1940), 49.
35. William Forbes Adams, *Ireland and Irish Emigration to the New World From 1815 to the Famine*. (New Haven, Conn.: Yale University Press, 1932), 65.
36. David Noel Doyle, *Ireland, Irishmen and Revolutionary America* (Dublin and Cork: The Mercier Press, 1981), 77.
37. Leyburn, *The Scotch-Irish,* 80–88.
38. Philip Robinson, *The Plantation of Ulster: British Settlement In An Irish Landscape, 1600–1670* (New York: St. Martin's Press, 1984), 46–47.
39. Ibid., 1.
40. Perceval-Maxwell, *The Scottish Migration*, 281.
41. Robinson, *The Plantation*, 4.
42. Robert Dunlop, "Sixteenth Century Schemes for the Plantation of Ulster," *Scottish Historical Review* 22 (October 1924–April 1925), 51.
43. Perceval-Maxwell, *The Scottish Migration*, 4.
44. Dunlop, "Sixteenth Century," 54.
45. Ibid.

46. Robinson, *The Plantation*, 5.

47. Dunlop, "Sixteenth Century," 113.

48. Ibid.

49. Ibid.

50. All these entrepreneurs in Ulster discovered that individual enterprises in Ireland were as difficult as those in America. Dunlop, "Sixteenth Century," 117–119. As is well known, Sir Walter Raleigh went bankrupt trying to make a go of the Roanoke Colony, off North Carolina, at about the same time as the various settlement schemes were being put forward in Ireland.

51. Dunlop, "Sixteenth Century," 123

52. Perceval-Maxwell, *The Scottish Migration*, 10.

53. Dunlop, "Sixteenth Century," 124.

54. Dunlop, "Sixteenth Century," 199–200; Robinson, *The Plantation*, 49.

55. Leyburn, *The Scotch-Irish*, 84.

56. See Jonathan Bardon, *Belfast: An Illustrated History* (Dundonald, Ireland: Blackstaff Press, 1982), 8–10. Chichester described the place: "The town of Bealfast is plotted out in a good forme, wherein are many fameleys of English, Scotch, and osmoe Manksmen, already inhabitinge, of which some are artificers who have buylte good tymber houses, with chimneys after the fashion of the English palle, and one inn with very good Lodginge which is a great comfort to the travellers in those parts." Bardon, 13.

57. Leyburn, *The Scotch-Irish*, 84–88.

58. Arthur Chichester, Letter to Governor of Carrickfergus; 24 October 1606, (Belfast: Public Records Office, Northern Ireland). Hereafter referred to as PRONI.

59. Arthur Chichester, Letter to the Sheriff of Coleraine, 13 September 1607. PRONI.

60. Bardon, *Belfast*, 12; Robinson, *The Plantation*, 37–43.

61. Deputies and Commissioners of Armagh, Letter to Arthur Chichester, 18 July 1608, PRONI.

62. Lord Deputy of Armagh, Letter to Sir Arthur Chichester, 18 July 1608, PRONI.

63. David Beers Quinn, *The Elizabethans and the Irish* (Ithaca, N.Y.: Cornell University Press, 1966), 14–15.

64. Lord Deputy of Armagh, Letter to Sir Arthur Chichester; 18 July 1608, PRONI.

65. Ibid.

66. Leyburn, *The Scotch-Irish,* 47.

67. Ibid.

68. Perceval-Maxwell, *The Scottish Migration,* 55.

69. Ibid., 84.

70. Leyburn, *The Scotch-Irish*, 93.

71. See Rick Bromer, "The Scotch-Irish," *Susquehanna*, (December, 1986); 18–23. Also Perceval-Maxwell, *The Scottish Migration*, 75–82.

72. Perceval-Maxwell, *The Scottish Migration*, 75.

73. Paul Lantz, "The Scotch-Irish in Pennsylvania," 1987 speech to Market Square Presbyterian Church, Harrisburg, Pennsylvania.

74. Robinson, *The Plantation*, 63.

75. Leyburn, *The Scotch-Irish*, 37.

76. Ibid.

77. Lantz speech, 1987.

78. Ibid.

79. Perceval-Maxwell, *The Scottish Migration*, 177.

80. Quinn, *The Elizabethans*, 121.

81. Robinson, *The Plantation*, 1.

82. Percevel-Maxwell, *The Scottish Migration*, 126.

83. Robinson, *The Plantation*, 129.

84. Perceval-Maxwell, *The Scottish Migration*, 152.

85. Irish State Papers, File 615/4; PRONI.

86. Robinson, *The Plantation*, 110.

87. Notestein, *The Scots in History*, 142.

88. Irish State Papers, File 615/4, PRONI.

89. Ibid.

90. Richard Hofstadter, *Anti-Intellectualism in American Life* (New York: Alfred A. Knopf, 1963), 272–273.

CHAPTER TWO

1. Bromer, "The Scotch-Irish," 20.

2. Ibid.

3. Isabel Montgomrie, Letter to Earl of Rochester; 24 September 1638, PRONI.

4. Military Report, 1645, PRONI.

5. Klein, "The Scotch-Irish," 30–36.

6. Maude Glascow, *The Scotch-Irish in Northern Ireland And In The American Colonies* (New York: G. P. Putnam's Sons, 1936), 43–80. Also Bromer, "The Scotch-Irish," 20.

7. Bromer, "The Scotch-Irish," 20.
8. Citizen, Letter to the Commissioners of Ulster; 7 March 1645, PRONI.
9. Petition to Commissioners of Ulster; 31 March 1646, PRONI.
10. Commission Response to Petition of 31 March 1646, PRONI.
11. Ibid.
12. Klein, "The Scotch-Irish," 35.
13. Robinson, "The Plantation," 37.
14. Ibid.
15. Leyburn, *The Scotch-Irish*, 117.
16. Robinson, *The Plantation*, 29.
17. Ibid. 139
18. Thomas Wyllie, Letter to Ballymoney Presbyterians, 9 January 1672, PRONI.
19. Thomas Wyllie, Letters to Ballymoney Presbyterians, 27 February 1672; 10 March 1672, PRONI.
20. David Houstoune, Letter to the Ballymoney Presbyterians, 23 August 1671, PRONI.
21. Wyllie Letter to Balleymoney Presbyterians; 10 March 1672, PRONI.
22. Richard Hofstadter, "The Coming of the Americans," *American History Illustrated*, 6:6 (October, 1971), 34.
23. Anna Adams Dickie, "Scotch-Irish Presbyterian Settlers in Southern Wisconsin," *The Wisconsin Magazine of History* 31:3 (March 1948), 292.
24. Possibly this battle is still the most remembered event among the Ulster Protestants who stayed in north Ireland and did not immigrate to America. Each year the anniversary of the Battle of the Boyne occasions huge commemorative parades in the major cities of Ulster, especially Belfast. The day is always one of tension as the Protestants celebrate their victory to the consernation of Catholics in the area. Often, the anniversary leads to terrible clashes between these two sets of Christians who seem to have nothing but loathing for each other.
25. Bishop of Down petitioning the Lords Justices of Ireland; September 1698, PRONI.
26. Ibid.
27. Dickie, "Scotch-Irish," 298.
28. Presbyterian Ministers and People in the North of Ireland petitioning the Lord Lieutenant General and General Government of the Kingdom of Ireland, n.d., 1690.

29. As late as 1934, some Presbyterian churches were still having problems with the Church of England over the matter of sacraments. The Kirk of British Honduras (now Belize) suffered numerous financial setbacks in the 1930s and it asked the Anglicans for help. The latter were willing, but for a price. Baptisms and burials could be performed according to the rites of the Church of Scotland; the sacrament of communion, however, must adhere to Anglican forms and practices. The Bishop of the West Indies, Arthur Dunn, wrote to the Clerk of Sessions of the Presbyterian Church in Belize City, Wilson MacMillan (later, Sir Wilson) that he (Dunn) had conferred with Anglican Church officials, and that they adamantly insisted on Church of England sacraments.

One member of the Belize Church wrote: "Their [Church of England] form of worship . . . was high . . . very high, whereas the Scotch Church form was low—very low—and was it possible for the two extremes to meet?" Apparently, the answer to that question was "no," for the Kirk in Belize City unanimously declined Bishop Dunn's offer.

The Belize Kirk then turned to the Methodists for help in finances and supplying ministers. Methodism was closer to Presbyterianism than the latter to Anglicanism. The Methodists, moreover, did not make sacramental demands of the Presbyterians as the Anglicans had done. Record, Presbyterian Church, Belize City, Belize; Central America. The author is indebted to the Reverend Robert Watts for access to these records.

30. Hofstadter, "The Coming," 35.

31. Drogheda Presbyterians memorializing the English Parliament, 1702, PRONI.

32. Drogheda Presbyterian Report, October, 1708, PRONI.

33. Ibid.

34. Ibid.

35. Narcissus, Archbishop of Armagh, Letter to the English Parliament, 1708, PRONI.

36. Ibid.

37. Ibid.

38. Hofstadter, "The Coming," 34.

39. Ibid.

40. *The Irish Proposals In Report of Commissioners of Trade and Plantation of The English Woollen and Irish Linen Manufactures*, File 615/4, PRONI.

41. Ibid.

42. See M. G. Jones, *The Charity School Movement: A Study of Eighteenth Century Puritanism in Action* (Cambridge: Cambridge University Press, 1938), 226.
43. Bromer, "The Scotch-Irish," 20.
44. Dickie, "Scotch-Irish," 291.
45. Bromer, "The Scotch-Irish," 20; Leyburn, *The Scotch-Irish*, 162; Leyburn, "The Scotch-Irish," 98.
46. Leyburn, "The Scotch-Irish," 98.

CHAPTER THREE

1. Bardon, *Belfast*, 32.
2. Howard Cromie, *Ulster Settlers in America* (Belfast: Universities Press, 1976), 14–16.
3. Ibid. 31–32.
4. Ibid.
5. Ibid.
6. Ibid.
7 Maury Klein, "The Nation-Builders," I, *American History Illustrated*, 13: 10, (February, 1979): 32.
8. Leyburn, *The Scotch-Irish*, 237.
9. According to an article in the *Magazine of American History*, March, 1883, an Ulster colony was projected in New England as early as 1638. The article stated that 140 passengers sailed from Loch Fergus, but were driven back by the weather, and "nearly three-quarters a century elapsed before we hear of the arrival of the Scotch-Irish in the New England colonies."
10. Memorandum and Journal of William Cauldwell, 9 June 1829, Wilson Whitehead Collection, Bowling Green, Kentucky.
11. David Cressy, *Coming Over: Migration and Communication Between England and New England in the Seventeenth Century* (Cambridge: Cambridge University Press, 1987), 147. See also Guy Soulliard Klett, *Presbyterians In Colonial Pennsylvania* (Philadelphia: University of Pennsylvania Press, 1937), 25.
12. Cressy, *Coming Over*, 151.
13. E. R. R. Green, ed., "Ulster Immigrant Letters," *Essays in Scotch-Irish History* (London: Routledge and Kegan Paul, 1984), 93.
14. Quite often the Scotch-Irishman's mind to sail was made up by the brochures sent out by numerous ship companies. Malcolm & Bell of Donegall Quay in Belfast, sent notice of a passage to Alexander

Cauldwell, and at the same time informed him that "if any of your friends or neighbors wish to go to AMERICA the present [1834] is a desirable opportunity. The Vessels consigned to us, are of the first class, and commanded by kind and experienced captains. We shall continue the same punctuality as heretofore, of sailing the Ships on the day named. . . ." Maintaining a steady public relations effort, the company promised the inhabitants of Scotland and Ulster to take all their letters for friends and families in America, and "forward immediately, without charge." Ship's Advertisement, Whitehead Collection, Bowling Green, Kentucky.

15. Charles Livingston, Letter to Duncan Gibb, 12 July 1822, Livingston Papers, Duke University, Durham, North Carolina.

16. Ibid. One ship that got stranded on its way from Belfast was the *Alexis*. She was "forced on a shoal near the main bar by a sudden breeze."

17. Klein, "The Nation-Builders," I, 32.

18. E. R. R. Green, "The Strange Humors That Drove The Scotch-Irish To America, 1729," *William and Mary Quarterly* 12 (1955), 113.

19. Guy S. Klett, Presbyterians In Colonial Pennsylvania (Philadelphia: University of Pennsylvania Press, 1937), 20.

20. R. J. Dickson, *Ulster Immigration To Colonial America* (London: Routledge and Kegan Paul, 1966), 21.

21. Lord Carteret reporting to Duke of Newcastle, 26 June 1729, File 659, State Papers, Ireland, PRONI.

22. Ibid.

23. Green, "Strange Humors," 116–17.

24. Green, "Strange Humors," 117, 122, 123.

25. Edward Moor receipt to Hugh Scott, 25 May 1825, from papers in the possession of Mrs. Mary Alice Cooper, Avonmore, Pa.

26. Story told by Reverend Thomas S. Naylor Todd, in the collection of Nancy M. Cladel, Hummelstown, Pa.

27. William James Young, Letter to his mother, 24 June 1831, in the papers of S. R. Hunter, Stoneboro, Pa.

28. Ibid.

29. Ibid.

30. John Craig Autobiography, in the Collection of the Presbyterian Historical Foundation, Montreat, North Carolina.

31. Ibid.

32. Jonathan Moore Diary, 21 May 1760, PRONI.

33. William James Young Diary, 17 July 1832. Not everything on these crossings had a morbid flavor. Moore wrote: "It is wonderful

to see birds in the ocean so far from any land. . . . There are generally two kinds, one resembling a wild duck called sheer waters, five or six kinds of them; the other sort is called a bittern which very much resembles a swallow. They almost continually fly about the vessel in great numbers, especially if it blows fresh. Sometimes there is such number of porpoises tumbling that they appear like a great party." Moore Diary, May-June, 1760. Moore saw grampuses, or small whales, spouting water into the air, and "some of them looked to be half as long as the vessel." He marveled at the "needle impregnated with the mechanical virtue to enable the navigator . . . to bring a vessel 3,000 miles through the spacious, wide ocean within a few miles of the intended course." Ibid.

34. Moore Diary, May-June 1760, PRONI.

35. *Belfast Newsletter*, April 29, 1750. The *Belfast News Letter*, today the oldest continuous English language newspaper in existence, frequently served as a conduit between immigrants and friends and family back home in Ulster. Francis Jay and sons ran the newspaper for years on Bridge Street in Belfast, and called it *The Belfast Newsletter and General Advertiser*. Later, the two brothers, Henry and Robert, published it. Some time after the 1750s, its name was shortened to *Belfast Newsletter*.

36. Mary Alice Cooper of Avonmore, Pa., Letter to the author 30 May 1987.

37. Young Diary, 10 July, 1832.

38. Young Diary, 2 August 1832.

39. Ibid, 3 August 1832.

40. R. J. Dickson quoting John Daniel Crimmins, *The Irish-American Historical Miscellany* (New York: The Author, 1905), 21. Also, Henry Jones Ford, *The Scotch-Irish in America* (New York: Arno Press, 1969), 207.

41. Ibid.

42. *Belfast Newsletter*, 9 March 1762.

43. Robert Smilie, Letter to his father, 11 November 1762. Published in the *Belfast Newsletter*, 13 May 1763, PRONI. The entire letter was reprinted in Dickson, *Ulster Immigration*, 287–90.

44. Ibid. Also Bardon, *Belfast*, 33.

45. R. J. Dickson, *Ulster Immigration*, 287–90.

46. Young Diary, 14 August 1832.

47. Dickie, "Scotch-Irish Presbyterian," 299.

48. Alexander Chesney Diary, August-October 1772, PRONI.

49. Ibid.

50. Ibid.
51. Hofstadter, "The Coming," 47.

CHAPTER FOUR

1. Doyle, *Ireland*, 82.
2. George H. Smyth, "The Scotch-Irish in New England," *Magazine of American History*, IX: 3, (March 1883), 153.
3. Leyburn, *The Scotch-Irish*, 241.
4. Hofstadter, "The Coming," 43.
5. Klein, "The Nation Builders," I: 34.
6. Ibid.
7. Cromie, *Ulster Settlers*, 16; Hofstadter, "The Coming," 43.
8. Leyburn, "The Scotch-Irish," 30.
9. Hofstadter, "The Coming," 43.
10. Klein, "The Nation Builders," I: 34.
11. Leyburn, *The Scotch-Irish*, 241.
12. Hofstadter, "The Coming," 44.
13. Ibid. Also Smyth, "Scotch-Irish in New England," 154.
14. This was, of course, the reintroduction of potatoes to the New World. Columbus had taken potato plants back to the Old World, and they succeeded in the soils of Ireland. To this day, the early 1990s, there are still certain people in the United States who refer to this vegetable as "Irish potatoes."
15. Smyth, "Scotch-Irish in New England," 156.
16. Ibid.
17. Ibid., 157.
18. Ibid., 164.
19. Gary Nash, *The Urban Crucible: Social Change, Political Consciousness, and the Origins of the American Revolution* (Cambridge, Mass: Harvard University Press, 1979), 103.
20. Ibid. 105.
21. Cromie, *Ulster Settlers*, 19.
22. Russell A. Patton of Columbia, Pa., Letter to the author, 10 February 1987.
23. Robert L. Clark, comp., *A History Of The Presbytery of Westminster And Its Antecedents 1732–1924* (Privately published, date unknown), 2–3.
24. Bardon, *Belfast*, 31.
25. Cromie, *Ulster Settlers*, 16.

26. Klein, "The Nation-Builders," I:36.

27. Ibid.

28. Ibid.

29. Mary E. Karnes, "Donegal Presbyterian Church," *Lancaster County Heritage*, 1:1, (July 1984), 104.

30. Ibid.

31. George D. Wolf, *The Fair Play Settlers of the West Branch Valley, 1769–1784: A Study of Frontier Ethnography*, (Harrisburg, Pa: Privately published, 1969) 122. Cromie, *Ulster Settlers*, 18.

32. Cromie, *Ulster Settlers*, 21. See also Kerby A. Miller, *Emigrants and Exiles: Ireland and the Irish Exodus to North America* (New York: Oxford University Press, 1985), 167, for a discussion of how the American Revolution caused the Scotch-Irish to "justly claim" the title, "American."

33. Ibid.

34. Ibid, 16.

35. K. Edward Lay, "European Antecedents of Seventeenth and Eighteenth Century Germanic and Scots-Irish Architecture in America," *Pennsylvania Folklife*, 32:1 (Autumn 1982): 34.

36. Karnes, "Donegal," 105.

37. Ibid.

38. Ibid.

39. Ibid. 107.

40. *Middle Spring Church: A History* (n.p., n.d), 26–27. Copy in the paper of William H. Burkhart, Shippensburg, Pa.

41. Cromie, *Ulster Settlers*, 29.

42. *A Session Book For The Use Of The Session Of The Congregation Of Middle Spring*. The first entry in this session book was 27 December 1742 and the last one 8 February 1749. The author was allowed to use this sessions book on the understanding that he would not divulge the full names of any of the parties involved; hence, the initials. I am indebted to the Reverend David E. Longacre of Star Route Two, Shippensburg, Pa., for his assistance in acquiring these records.

43. Chalmers G. Davidson, *The Colonial Scotch-Irish of the Carolina Piedmont* (Richburg and Chester, S.C.: Chester County Genealogical Society and Chester Historical Society, 1979), 11.

44. Cromie, *Ulster Settlers*, 30.

45. *Middle Spring Sessions Book*, 2 May 1743.

46. Ibid.

47. Ibid. 5 September 1743.

48. Ibid., 4 February, no year given.

49. Ibid., 18 July 1746.

50. This altercation occurred in October 1743; the Middle Spring session dealt with it at its January 1744 meeting.

51. Hofstadter, "The Coming," 36.

52. See Clarke Thomas, "Presbyterian Pittsburgh," *Pittsburgh Post-Gazette*, 18 February 1987.

53. Lay, "European Antecedents, 2.

54. Ibid.

55. Ibid.

CHAPTER FIVE

1. Leyburn, *The Scotch-Irish*, 199.

2. In 1987 Nancy Baxter of Indianapolis published a novel titled *The Movers*. It started out in Londonderry, northern Ireland, with a young Scotch-Irishman, John McClure, making hasty plans to come to America after he had accidentally killed someone. It ended with the Battle of Tippecanoe in Indiana, when General William Henry Harrison defeated the Shawnees. In the book, Miss Baxter talks at length about some of the earliest Scotch-Irish families in America, including the McClures and the Bards. *The Movers* is the first volume of a series of books to be published by Miss Baxter, called The Heartland Chronicles. The publisher is Guild Press of Indiana.

3. James T. Lemon, *The Best Poor Man's Country: A Geographical Study of Early Southeastern Pennsylvania* (Baltimore and London: The Johns Hopkins University Press, 1972), 71.

4. Doyle, *Ireland*, 82.

5. This statement of James Logan, 23 October 1730, was quoted in *The Centennial Memorial of the Presbytery of Carlisle*, (Carlyle, Pa.: Myers Printing and Publishing House, 1889), I: 49. Augusta County Public Library, Staunton, Virginia.

6. Clifford Neale Smith, *Typescript*, 3–4. Pennsylvania Historical Society; Philadelphia, Pennsylvania.

7. Allen, Armagh, Carlisle, Derry, Eastpennsburgh, Fermanagh, Greenwood, Hopewell, Lack, Middleton, Millford, Newton, Rye, Shippensberg, Tyrone, Tobayne, Westpennsborough, and Wayne.

8. Israel Daniel Rupp, *The History and Topography of Dauphin, Cumberland, Franklin, Bedford, Adams, and Perry Counties* (Lancaster, Pa.: Gilbert Hills, 1846), 1–20; Also Smith *Typescript*, 3–4.

9. Lamberton Papers, Pennsylvania Historical Society. Also see *Virginia Magazine of History and Biography*, vol. 18; 40.

10. Moore Diary, 1762(?) PRONI.

11. Ibid.

12. Job Johnston, Letter to his brothers, 27 November 1767, PRONI.

13. Ibid.

14. Ibid.

15. Ibid.

16. James Murray, Letter to the Reverend Baptist Boyd, 1737. PRONI. This letter was reproduced in the *Pennsylvania Gazette*, 27 October 1737.

17. Ibid.

18. Ibid.

19. Zachariah Butcher, Letter to the Governor, 1741, Pennsylvania Archives, 1st Series, 1: 625, Balch Institute, Philadelphia, Pennsylvania.

20. Parke Rouse, *The Great Philadelphia Wagon Road: From Philadelphia To The South* (New York: McGraw-Hill, 1973), 23.

21. Lantz speech, 1987.

22. Parke Rouse's book, *The Great Philadelphia Wagon Road,* discussed *all* immigrants, including the Scotch-Irish, who used that road for their journeys down into the Carolinas and to Georgia, Tennessee, and Kentucky.

23. Rouse, *Wagon Road*, 33.

24. Ernest Trice Thompson, *Presbyterians In The South, 1607–1861* (Richmond, Va.: John Knox Press, 1963), I: 45. Also Benjamin Rice Lacy, Jr. *Revivals In The Midst Of The Years* (Richmond, Va.: John Knox Press, 1943), 37–44.

25. Elizabeth House (Mrs. Nicholas Trist) Diary; 26 December 1783 to 1 July 1784, Southern Collection, University of North Carolina, Chapel Hill, North Carolina.

26. Ibid.

27. Sally Hastings, *A Descriptive Account Of A Family Tour To The West, In The Year 1800 In A Letter To A Lady* (Lancaster, Pa.: William Dickson, Printers, 1808), 177–209. In the collections of Mary E. Karnes, Elizabethtown, Pa.

28. Ibid.

29. Ibid.

30. Ibid.

31. Richard R. Beeman, *The Evolution Of The Southern Backcoun-*

try: A Case Study of Lunenburg County, Virginia, 1746–1832 (Philadelphia: University of Pennsylvania Press, 1984), 99.

32. Ibid., 23.

33. Alan Crozier, "The Scotch-Irish Influence on American English," *American Speech*, 59:4 (1984): 319.

34. Davidson, *Colonial Scotch-Irish*, 10.

35. Carl Bridenbaugh, *Myths and Realities: Societies of the Colonial South* (Baton Rouge: Louisiana State University Press, 1952), 184.

36. J. Houston Harrison, *Settlers By The Long Grey Trail: A Contribution To The History and Genealogy Of Colonial Families Of Rockingham County, Virginia* (Baltimore: Genealogical Publishing, 1875), 114.

37. Cromie, *Ulster Settlers*, 25. See also Harold McKnight Wilson, *The Lexington Presbytery Heritage* (Verona, Va.: McClure Press, 1971), 17.

38. Lyman Chalkley, *Chronicles of The Scotch-Irish Settlement in Virginia, Extracted From The Original Court Records of Augusta County, 1745–1800* (Baltimore: Genealogical Publishing, 1974), I: 17, 19, 20.

39. Ibid.

40. An additional example of how the Augusta County Court looked after the public welfare was during the American Revolution. In March, 1777, the court considered the "advisability of inoculations" for smallpox. It decided that physicians be given the smallpox preventatives, while any person within a three mile radius of places where the disease raged could likewise receive the treatment. The court ordered that those stricken with the disease be isolated from healthy persons. The sheriff of Augusta County was empowered by the court to enforce these directives. Chalkley, *Chronicles*, 190.

41. Chalkley, *Chronicles*, 205, 235.

42. Ibid.

43. Davidson, *Colonial Scotch-Irish*, 1–2.

44. Ibid., 3.

45. Board of Trade Folder, 1736, PRONI.

46. *Belfast Newsletter*, 26 June 1753.

47. Forrest McDonald and Grady McWhiney, "The Antebellum Southern Herdsman: A Reinterpretation." *The Journal of Southern History*, XLI: 2 (May 1975), 152–53.

48. Ibid.

49. McWhiney gained some attention with his thesis a few years

ago dealing with the Celtic influence in settling British North America. See Grady McWhiney and Perry D. Jamieson, *Attack And Die: Civil War Military Tactics And The Southern Heritage* (University, Ala.: University of Alabama Press, 1982).

50. John MacLellan Family Papers, Folder, Winthrop College, Rock Hill, South Carolina.

51. Ibid.

52. Southern Wisconsin, for example, has a large settlement of Scotch-Irish in Lima and Kashkonony townships, who came directly from Ballymacombs in Ulster. In Wisconsin these Scotch-Irish joined with other emigrant groups, notably the Germans, in making their state one of the most agriculturally productive in the union.

CHAPTER SIX

1. Daniel Rupp, *An Original History of the Religious Denominations at Present Existing in the United States* (Philadelphia: J. Y. Humphries, 1844), 202.

2. Elizabeth Nybakken, "New Light on the Old Side," *Journal of American History* 68 (1982), 813–32.

3. Some scholars have compared the emotion and enthusiasm of the New Siders with Born Again Christianity of our own time.

4. Marilyn J. Westerkamp, *Triumph of the Laity: Scots-Irish Piety and the Great Awakening, 1625–1760* (New York: Oxford University Press, 1988), 14.

5. Ibid., 168.

6. Davidson, *Colonial Scotch-Irish*, 8–9.

7. Alexander Craighead, "Renewing the Covenant," 11 November 1743, Craighead Papers, Historical Foundation, Montreat, North Carolina.

8. Ibid.

9. Ibid. An antiprelatic was opposed to church government by bishops and other high ranking authorities; antiErastians opposed the state being involved in church matters; and an antilatitudinarian opposed those who cared little about religious forms and creeds.

10. Ibid. Independency was the idea that a local church should be self-sufficient and not depend for its well being on an external ecclesiastical authority; Libertinism was made up of people who led unrestrained lives; the Anabaptists, among other things, opposed infant baptism; Antinomians believed that faith alone, not adherence

to a moral law, was necessary for salvation; Arminians stressed free will rather than predestination; Socinians denied the divinity of Jesus and explained sin and salvation from a rational point of view; and the Moravians represented the doctrines of John Huss as taught in Moravia. A part of their beliefs was the supremacy of scripture.

11. Herbert S. Turner, *Bethel And Her Ministers, 1746–1946* (H. S. Turner, 1946), 21.

12. Ernest Craighead, "Craighead Ministers in Ulster and Colonial America," undated, Presbyterian Historical Society, Philadelphia, Pennsylvania.

13. Craig *Autobiography*, in the Collection of the Presbyterian Historical Foundation, Montreat, North Carolina.

14. Ibid.

15. Rhea Family Papers, Folder 1, Historical Foundation; Montreat, North Carolina.

16. Ibid.

17. Moore Diary, 1762 (?) PRONI.

18. William McCash, "Jonathan Edwards: A Study of the Influences on New England's Foremost Philosopher," (Unpublished paper, University of Georgia, 1960), 27.

19. Moore Diary, PRONI.

20. Ibid.

21. Weir Papers, Folder I, 1770s, PRONI.

22. Ibid.

23. Ibid.

24. James E. Johnson, *The Scots and Scotch-Irish In America* (Minneapolis: Lerner Publications, 1966), 35.

25. Cromie, *Ulster Settlers*, 28.

26. Ibid.

27. William C. Lehmann, *Scottish and Scotch-Irish Contributions to Early American Life and Culture*, 2d ed. (Washington, D.C.: Lehmann-Spohr, 1980), 85.

28. Edward Scott Gaustad, *The Great Awakening in New England* (New York: Harper, 1957), 134.

29. Reflecting the controversies, the New Side Synod of New York was created. It joined in 1758 with the older, Philadelphia Synod, "a union of oil and water," as one minister described it. Rhea Family Papers, Historical Foundation; Montreat, North Carolina. In the early 1770s the two synods broke apart because of the constant "browbeating, contempt, and unchristian quarrels" that had occurred in the past dozen years. Ibid. By 1789, however, the two factions had once

again united because in that year the Presbyterian General Assembly met in Philadelphia. During the Civil War, 1861–1865, the church split into northern and southern branches. It was not until 1983 that these two factions got back together. Today, the national headquarters for the Presbyterians in the United States is in Louisville, Kentucky.

30. Nybakken, "New Light," 815.

31. Rhea Family Papers, Folder 1, 1770s, Historical Foundation, Montreat, North Carolina. If the moon always stayed on course from west to east, Rhea said, tides would ebb and flow twice every day at exactly the same time, "because the earth turning around would bring the same part of the sea under the moon every twenty-four hours." But the moon advances every day by twelve degrees. Thus, "the earth must go as far (twelve degrees) before the lower part of the surface of the sea be brought under the moon again." This phenomenon, he said, explained why each tide is ninety minutes beyond its predecessor of twelve hours before.

32. John Craig Collection, Historical Foundation; Montreat, North Carolina.

33. Cromie, *Ulster Settlers*, 35.

34. Harold McKnight Wilson, *The Lexington Presbytery Heritage*. (Verona, Virginia: McClure Press, 1971), 82. Well into the twentieth century, the teachers at high schools around the country were called "professors." This "dialogue" took place one time between a "professor" and a student :

Prof. "What's your name?"
Student. "Stillman A. Darrell, Sir."
Prof. "Scotch-Irish?"
Student. "Yes sir."
Prof. "You may go now, but don't let it happen again, Darrell."
Stillman A. Darrell, Jr. of West Chester, Pa., Letter to the author, 23 February 1987.

35. Cromie, *Ulster Settlers*, 36.

36. Ibid.

37. Ibid.

38. Lantz speech, 1987.

39. Leyburn, "The Scotch-Irish," 100.

40. Cromie, *Ulster Settlers*, 40.

41. Lantz Speech, 1987.

42. Davidson, *Colonial Scotch-Irish*, 8.

43. Lay, "European Antecedents," 18.

44. Johnson, *The Scots*, 42.

45. Ibid.
46. Klein, "The Nation-Builders," 111, 8.
47. Davidson, *Colonial Scotch-Irish*, 7.
48. Ibid.
49. Ibid.
50. Johnson, *The Scots*, 38. Lay, "European Antecedents," 3.
51. Doyle, *Ireland*, 87.
52. Edward Pessen, *Jacksonian America; Society, Personality, and Politics*. rev. ed. (Homewood, Ill.: Dorsey Press, 1978), 105–106.
53. Johnson, *The Scots*, 42.
54. Davidson, *Colonial Scotch-Irish*, 14–15.
55. Ibid.
56. Doyle, *Ireland*, 88.
57. Davidson, *Colonial Scotch-Irish*, 15–16.
58. Elizabeth Weir, Letter to "My Very Dear Uncle." n.d., Weir Family Papers, PRONI.
59. Certificate of Marriage, Hugh Scott and Margret Varuit; 6 August 1818, in the papers of Nancy M. Cladel, Hummelstown, Pa.
60. Johnson, *The Scots*, 43.
61. Ibid.
62. Davidson, *Colonial Scotch-Irish*, 15.
63. Klein, "The Nation-Builders," 111:12.
64. Alan Crozier, "The Scotch-Irish Influence On American English," *American Speech*, 59:4 (1984): 310.
65. Ibid., 326.
66. Russell A. Patton of Columbia, Pa., telephone conversation with the author, 1 November 1988.
67. Mary Alice Cooper of Avonmore, Pa., Letter to the author, 30 May 1987.
68. From the Collections of Nancy Cladel; Hummelstown, PA.
69. Cromie, *Ulster Settlers*, 25–26.
70. Ibid., 27.
71. Craig Diary, August 1737, Historical Foundation, Montreat, North Carolina.
72. *Belfast Newsletter*, 5 April 1754.
73. *Belfast Newsletter*, 17 October 1755.
74. Ibid.
75. Letter to the *Belfast Newsletter*; 9 January 1756.
76. *Belfast Newsletter*, 5 February 1756.
77. Guy S. Klett, *Presbyterians In Colonial Pennsylvania* (Philadelphia: University of Pennsylvania Press, 1937), 252–54.

78. Lantz speech, 1987. Bromer, "The Scotch-Irish," 22–23. Klein, "The Nation-Builders," II: 23.

79. John Garraty, *The American Nation: A History of the United States* (New York: Harper & Row, 1966), 100–101. See also Klett, *Presbyterians*, 252–54.

80. Doyle, *Ireland*, 122. One historian, as least, has connected the Paxton Boys to some of the religious questions current at that time. "The uprising of 'Paxton's Boys' . . . had no little to do with the ancient struggle between old and new side Presbyterians. . . ." See Alan Heimert, *Religion and the American Mind From the Great Awakening to the Revolution* (Cambridge: Harvard University Press, 1966), 381–382.

81. Bromer, "The Scotch-Irish," 23.

82. Sam Hunter, Stoneboro, Pa., Letter to the author, 20 April 1987.

CHAPTER SEVEN

1. *Heading for New Castle and Philadelphia: Rodger*, James Phillips, Master; *Prosperity*, William McCulloch; *Charlotte*, Thomas Egger; *Renown*, William Keith; *Peace and Plenty*, Charles McKenzie; *Liberty*, Thomas Lowdon; *Julina*, Robert Montgomery; *Minerva*, Charles Forrest; *Hannah*, James Ramage; *Recovery*, David McCullough; *The George*, William Pinkerton; *Brittania*, Samuel Kyle; *Betty and Hellen*, Patrick McCormack. *Heading for Baltimore: John* Charles Pooaug; *Lord Dunlace*, Robert Shutter; *Waddell*, William Scott. For New York: *James and Isabella,* John Moore; *Duke of Leinster,* Hugh Hamilton; *James and Mary*, John Manload. Some others that advertised periodically were *Nottingham*, *King of Prussia*, *Prince George*, *The Pitt*, *Marquis of Granbury*, *Culloden*, *Falls*, *Sally*, *George and Mary*, *Swanswick*, *Catherine*, *Terry*, *Two Sisters*, *Pallas*, *Hamilton Galley*, *Snow Hawke*, *Jenny*, *Nancy*, *Diamond*, *Ross*, *Lord Russell*, *William and James*, *William and Mary*, *Antrim*, *Upton*, *Bennett Galley* (which burned during a 1752 crossing), *Dursley Galley*, *The City of Derry*, *Henry*, *Nelly*, *Prince George*, and *Annabella*.

2. See Geoffrey Gorer, *The American People: A Study in National Character* rev. ed (New York: W. W. Norton, 1968), 27–29, for a discussion of how "un-English" the Parliament had become.

3. Doyle, *Ireland*, 131.

4. Doyle, *Ireland*, 133–4.

5. Cromie, *Ulster Settlers*, quoting Lord O'Neill, 48.

6. Cromie, *Ulster Settlers*, 45, 52. Also Klein, "The National-Builders," III, 15–16.

7. Quoted in Karnes, Donegal. np.

8. Klein, "The Nation-Builders," III: 16.

9. Quoted in Harold McKnight Wilson, *The Lexington Presbytery Heritage* (Verona, Pa.: McClure Press, 1971), 50.

10. Quoted in Ernest Trice Thompson, *Presbyterians in The South, 1607–1861* (Richmond, Va.: John Knox Press, 1963), 92.

11. Lehmann, *Scottish*, 100.

12. James T. Lemon, *The Best Poor Man's Country: A Geographical Study of Early Southeastern Pennsylvania* (Baltimore and London: The John Hopkins Press, 1972), 21.

13. Doyle, *Ireland*, 136.

14. John Butler, Letter to William Butler; 2 August 1772, Southern Collection, University of North Carolina, Chapel Hill, North Carolina.

15. Kerby A. Miller, *Emigrants and Exiles: Ireland and the Irish Exodus to North America* (New York: Oxford University Press, 1985), 165–66.

16. Joseph P. O'Grady, *How The Irish Became American* (New York: Twayne, 1973), 23.

17. Miller, *Emigrants*, 165–6.

18. Cromie, *Ulster Settlers*, 45–8.

19. From a history of the Todd Family, in the papers of Mary Alice Cooper, Avonmore, Pa.

20. Quoted in Thomas L. Preston, *Historical Sketches and Reminiscences of an Octogenarian* (Richmond: B. F. Johnson, 1900), 27–28; and George Bancroft, *History of the United States of America* (Boston: Little, Brown & Co., 1879), IV, 443–44.

21. Quoted by Howard McKnight Wilson, *The Tinkling Springs: Headwaters of Freedom* (Fisherville, Va.; Privately published, 1954), 189. Also *Washington and Lee University Papers* (Baltimore: John Murphy, 1890–1895), III; 33–34.

22. Thompson, *Presbyterians In The South*, 89–90. Also Joseph A. Waddell, *Annals of Augusta County Virginia* (Richmond: J. W. Randolph and English, 1886), 148–49.

23. From Mecklenburg Declaration, 19 May 1775. Southern Collection, University of North Carolina, Chapel Hill, North Carolina.

24. U.S. Declaration of Independence, 4 July 1776.

25. References to this idea are scattered throughout the Mecklen-

burg File in the Southern Collection at the University of North Carolina, Chapel Hill.

26. Jared Sparks, Letter to University of North Carolina President Swain, 14 January 1845. Southern Collection, University of North Carolina, Chapel Hill.

27. Craighead Collection, July 1766, Presbyterian Historical Society, Philadelphia, Pennsylvania.

28. Some historians over the years have expressed doubts that the Mecklenburg Declaration of Independence ever existed. It was claimed that the original document was burned in a fire in 1800. Critics, therefore, argued that there was no signed copy of the document with a date prior to 1800. There were three copies of the Declaration bearing the later date, yet each differed from the other in wording and even signers. Finally, the critics could find no accounts of the creation of the document in contemporary records such as newspapers and diaries. See notation by Charles Phillips, 24 November 1857, Southern Collection, University of North Carolina, Chapel Hill.

29. Marc Egnal, *A Mighty Empire: The Origins of the American Revolution* (Ithaca: Cornell University Press, 1988), 305.

30. Alexander McWhorter Papers; Southern Collection, University of North Carolina, Chapel Hill, North Carolina.

31. Margaret Duncan, Letter to William Weir; December, 1774. PRONI.

32. Ibid.

33. Ibid.

34. Jonathan Moore Diary. PRONI.

35. Ibid.

36. Johnson, *The Scots*, 33. Also Walter Brownlow Posey, *Frontier Missions: A History of Religion West of the Southern Appalachians to 1861* (Lexington: University of Kentucky Press, 1966), 10.

37. Cromie, *Ulster Settlers*, 45.

38. Quoted by Cromie, *Ulster Settlers*, 52.

39. Johnson, *The Scots*, 44–50. John Hancock was not an immigrant from Ulster, but his parents had come from County Down. Other Scotch-Irish who signed the Document were William Whipple, Robert Paine, Thomas McKean, Thomas Nelson, Matthew Thornton, George Taylor, and Edward Rutledge. The governors were Joshua Clayton, Delaware; George Walton, Georgia; John Howard, Maryland; Thomas Mifflin, Pennsylvania; Alexander Martin, North Carolina; William Livingston, New Jersey; John Sullivan, New Hamp-

shire; Beverly Randolph, Virginia; and Charles Pinckney, South Carolina.

40. Sibella Caldwell of Ulster, Letter to James Caldwell of Philadelphia, undated, PRONI.

41. Ibid.

42. *Belfast Newsletter*, 2–6 June 1775.

43. This advertisement first appeared in the *Belfast Newsletter* in August 1775, and continued every month or so for the next year.

44. *Belfast Newsletter*, in most of the 1776 fall issues.

45. Military journal of James Thatcher, August 1775, Copy in the papers of Mary Alice Cooper, Avonmore, Pa. Also Klein, "The Nation-Builders," III: 16.

46. John Armstrong Collection, Pennsylvania Historical Society, Philadelphia, Pennsylvania. Another important revolutionary leader in Pennsylvania was Alexander Lowrey. One Sunday morning in 1777 he and his men were attending services at the Donegal Presbyterian Church. A rider came with the message that British General William Howe was moving toward Philadelphia. Accordingly, Lowrey and his men left the church and assembled under a white oak tree, where they pledged anew their allegiance to the revolutionary cause. The oak thereafter was called "The Witness Tree." It was said that the pastor of Donegal Church at that time, the Reverend Colin McFarquhar, was not the most avid revolutionist among them. Therefore, he was forced by Lowrey's militiamen and the congregation to take off his hat and shout loudly for the patriot cause. It was said that in years to come, children played tricks on Reverend McFarquhar because of his supposed Loyalist sympathies during the Revolution. He wore a wig, and he usually assigned someone to shake talcum into it before he conducted a service. Once, some mischievous boys substituted powdered sugar for the usual talcum, with the result that the Reverend spent most of his sermon one Sunday morning chasing off flies. "Colin's Wig" became a part of the lore at Donegal Presbyterian Church. While these events may have occurred, it is almost for certain that the accounts of them are exaggerated. First, it is doubtful if any Presbyterian would rush out of church before hearing the benediction. Also, it seems clear that McFarquhar could not have remained at the church for over thirty years if he had been too much of a Tory. There are several accounts of the "Witness Tree" and "Colin's Wig." These come from Mary E. Karnes, *Donegal Presbyterian Church*, undated.

47. Cromie, *Ulster Scots*, 53–60. Also Thompson, *Presbyterians*

in the South, 91. One Scotch-Irish immigrant, Alexander Chesney (discussed in Chapter Four), remained loyal to the Crown. He was captured by revolutionary forces at King's Mountain, and forcibly "marched in an inclement season without either covering or provision except raw Indian corn to near the Moravian town on the northeast side of the Yadkin River." From this place, Chesney "most luckily and by a stratagem, made my escape . . . and got across the Yadkin River before morning." Chesney Diary, Fall, 1780, PRONI.

48. Kenneth Roberts, *The Battle of Cowpens: The Great Morale-Builder* (Garden City, N.J.: Doubleday, 1958), 19.

49. Egnal, *Mighty Empire*, 299.

50. Colonial Office Files, Folder 505, PRO, Kew, London, England.

51. Ibid.

52. Ibid., Also Colonial Office File 5678, PRO, Kew, London, England.

53. Miller, *Emigrants*, 167.

54. Leyburn, *The Scotch-Irish*, 317.

55. Robert L. Brunhouse, *The Counter-Revolution in Pennsylvania, 1776–1790* (New York: Octagon Books, 1971), 16.

56. Dorothy Voorhees, Scotch-Irish Society Registration Form, Balch Institute, Philadelphia, Pennsylvania.

57. Brunhouse, *Counter-Revolution*, 14.

58. Ibid.

59. Ibid.

60. Doyle, *Ireland*, 128.

61. Ibid.

62. This point is discussed by James G. Leyburn in his article, "The Scotch-Irish," 99.

63. See Doyle, *Ireland*, 192.

64. Leyburn, *The Scotch-Irish*, 314.

65. Klein, "The Nation-Builders," III: 16.

CHAPTER EIGHT

1. Diary, untitled and undated, Houstoun Collection, PRONI.

2. Maldwyn A. Jones, "Ulster Immigration, 1783–1815," *Essays in Scotch-Irish History*, (London: Routledge & Kegan Paul, 1969), 50.

3. Ibid.

4. Ibid.
5. Ibid.
6. Ibid.
7. Doyle, *Irish*, 81
8. Ibid.
9. Lay, "European Antecedents," 16.
10. Doyle, *Ireland*, 84.
11. Lemon, *Best Poor Man's Country*, 189.
12. Diary, Houstoun Collection, PRONI.
13. Ibid.
14. James Steele, Letter to Ephraim Steele, 5 March 1791; Steele Papers, Southern Collection, University of North Carolina, Chapel Hill, North Carolina.
15. James Steele, Letter to Ephraim Steele, 15 May 1797. Southern Collection, University of North Carolina. A few years later when England went to war with Napoleonic France, the cost of living, as well as taxes, shot up precipitously. James told Ephraim that some farms previously priced at twenty shillings an acre were now being sold for 20 per acre. Each wage earner, he said, had to pay a militia tax of fifteen shillings a year, a county tax of 3 14s a year, church tax, nine shillings a year, as well as additional sales taxes on all goods, which were particularly high on malt and whiskey. James Steele, Letter to Ephraim Steele, 24 April 1806. Southern Collection, University of North Carolina.
16. Ibid.
17. Caldwell Papers, 1797, PRONI.
18. Ibid.
19. Townsend Monckton Hall *Autobiography*, (Private, no date), Duke University, Durham, North Carolina. Other fierce battles included Wicklow, Dunlaven, Ocklaw, Bray, Blessingtown, White Heaps, Kilcullen Bridge, Red Lion, Killkenny, Cummins, Louth, Fermanagh, and Derry.
20. *Belfast Newsletter*, 22 May 1798.
21. Ibid.
22. John McMullen, Letter to Peter McMullen, 30 May 1799, McMullen Family Papers, Duke University.
23. Unknown person's Letter, Caldwell Papers, PRONI.
24. Ibid.
25. John Parks, Letter to John Caldwell, 3 August 1799. Caldwell Papers, PRONI.

26. John McMullen, Letter to Peter McMullen, 30 May 1799. McMullen Family Papers; Duke University.

27. J. Chambers, Letter to Robert Sims, 17 June 1807. Caldwell Papers, PRONI.

28. Silas Weir, Letter to James Robertson, 27 November 1795. Anderson Collection, PRONI.

29. John Caldwell, Letter to Robert Sims, 18 October 1802. Caldwell Papers, PRONI.

30. J. Chambers, Letter to Robert Sims, 17 June 1807. Caldwell Papers, PRONI.

31. Ibid.

32. Jones, *The Charity School Movement: A Study of Eighteenth Century Puritanism Action* (Cambridge: Cambridge University Press, 1938), 50–64.

33. Robert Given, Letter to John Given, 2 January 1821. Anderson Collection, PRONI.

34. John Campbell, Letter to Thomas Allen, 25 August 1819. Anderson Collection, PRONI.

35. John Anderson, Letter to his parents, 26 March 1837. Anderson Collection, PRONI.

36. James Weir, Letter to Elizabeth Weir, undated, Houstoun Collection, PRONI.

37. John Anderson to William Anderson, 6 September 1841. Anderson Collection, PRONI.

38. "Ulster Links With The White House," *Belfast Telegraph*, Collected Articles, undated, 19.

39. Chalmers G. Davidson, *The Colonial Scotch-Irish of the Carolina Piedmont* (Richburg and Chester, S.C.: Chester County Genealogical Society and Chester Historical Society, 1979), 6.

40. "Ulster Links," 45.

41. Cromie, *Ulster Settlers*, 57.

42. "Ulster Links," 3.

43. Bromer, "The Scotch-Irish," 23.

44. Pamphlet, Scotch-Irish Foundation, Balch Institute, Philadelphia.

Bibliography

PRIMARY SOURCES

Manuscript Collections

Balch Institute, Philadelphia, Pennsylvania:
Zachariah Butcher Letters, 1741.

Nancy M. Cladel Collection, Avonmore, Pennsylvania.

Mary Alice Cooper Collection, Avonmore, Pennsylvania.

Duke University Collections:
John McMullen Papers.
Livingston Papers.
Townsend Monckton Hall *Autobiography*.

S. R. Hunter Collection; Stoneboro, Pennsylvania.

Mary Karnes Collection, Elizabethtown, Pennsylvania.

John MacLellan Papers, Winthrop College, Rock Hill, South Carolina.

University of North Carolina Southern Collection:
John Butler Letters, 1772.
Elizabeth House Diaries.
Alexander McWhorter Papers.
Mecklenburg Papers.
Regulator Papers.
Jared Sparks Letters.
Ephraim Steele Papers, 1791–1806.

Pennsylvania Historical Society, Philadelphia, Pennsylvania:

John Armstrong Collection.
Lamberton Papers.
Clifford Neale Smith Paper.

Presbyterian Historical Foundation; Montreat, North Carolina:
John Craig Autobiography and Collection.
Alexander Craighead Collection.
Rhea Family Papers.

Presbyterian Historical Society, Philadelphia, Pennsylvania:
Ernest Craighead Collection.

Public Record Office, Kew, England:
Colonial Office Records, 1775–1777.

Public Records Office of North Ireland, Belfast, Northern Ireland:
John Anderson Collection.
James Caldwell Papers.
Alexander Chesney Diaries.
Houston Collection.

Irish State Papers, 1607, 1608, 1638, 1645, 1646, 1690, 1697, 1698, 1702, 1708, 1729.

Session Book For The Use of the Session of the Congregation of Middle Spring; Shippensburg, Pennsylvania.

Wilson Whitehead Collection, Private Collection, Bowling Green, Kentucky.

Secondary Sources

Articles in Periodicals and Newspapers

Belfast Newsletter, 1750–1800.

Bromer, Rick. "The Scotch-Irish," *Susquehannah*, (December 1986), 18–23.

Crozier, Alan. "The Scotch-Irish Influence on American English," *American Speech* 59: no. 4 (1984): 319.

Dickie, Anna Adams. "Scotch-Irish Presbyterian Settlers in Southern Wisconsin," *The Wisconsin Magazine of History,* 31, no. 3 (March, 1948): 292.

Dunlop, Robert. "Sixteenth Century Schemes For The Plantation of

Ulster," *Scottish Historical Review*, 22 (October, 1924–April, 1925): 51.

Green, E. R. R. "The 'Strange Humors' That Drove The Scotch-Irish To America, 1729,' *William and Mary Quarterly*, 12 (1955): 113–23.

——— "Ulster Immigrant Letters," in *Essays in Scotch-Irish History* (London: Routledge & Kegan Paul): 93.

Hofstadter, Richard. "The Coming of the Americans," *American History Illustrated*, 6, no. 6 (October, 1971): 4–11; 34; 47.

Hudson, Thomas F. "The Source of the Term Scotch-Irish," *Selected Proceedings of Scotch-Irish Heritage Festival II at Winthrop College* (November 17–19, 1983).

Klein, Maury. "The Nation-Builders," *American History Illustrated*, 13, no. 10 (February, 1979): 32.

——— "The Scotch-Irish: A Race in Upheaval," *American History Illustrated*, 13, no. 9 (January 1979): 30–36.

Karnes, Mary E. "Donegal Presbyterian Church," *Lancaster County Heritage*, 1, no. 1 (July 1984), 104.

Lay, Edward. "European Antecedents of Seventeenth and Eighteenth Century Germanic and Scots-Irish Architecture in America," *Pennsylvania Folklife*, 32, no. 1 (Autumn 1982): 34.

Lentz, Paul. "The Scotch-Irish in Pennsylvania," Speech, Market Square Presbyterian Church, Harrisburg, Pennsylvania, (1987). Pennsylvania.

McCash, William. "Jonathan Edwards: A Study of the Influences of New England's Foremost Philosopher," Unpublished paper, University of Georgia (1960).

McDonald, Forrest and McWhiney, Grady. "The Antebellum Southern Herdsman: A Reinterpretation," *The Journal of Southern History*, 41, no. 2 (May 1975): 152–153.

Nybakken, Elizabeth. "New Light on the Old Side," *Journal of American History* 68 (1982): 813–32.

Smythe, George H. "The Scotch-Irish in New England," *Magazine of American History*, 9, no. 3 (March 1883): 153.

Thomas, Clarke. "Presbyterian Pittsburgh," *Pittsburgh Post-Gazette*, 18 February 1987.

Books

Adams, William Forbes. *Ireland and Irish Emigration to the New World from 1815 to the Famine*. New Haven: Yale University Press, 1932. Discusses numbers of Scotch-Irish emigrations to the United States, especially after the War of 1812.

Bailyn, Bernard. *The Ideological Origins of the American Revolution*. Cambridge: Harvard University Press, 1967. Discusses the colonial (including the Scotch-Irish) aversion to standing armies.

——— *The Peopling of British North America: An Introduction*. New York: Random House, 1985. Discusses some of the movements of immigrants, especially the English and the Scotch, before they came to North America.

——— *Voyagers To The West: A Passage in the Peopling of America on the Eve of the Revolution*. New York: Random House, 1986. Uses the Register of Emigrants to study the vital statistics of people from England and Scotland who came to British North America in the years immediately preceding the American Revolution.

Bardon, Jonathan. *Belfast: An Illustrated History*. Dundonald: Blackstaff Press, 1982. Highly informative, scholarly, and useful book about Ulster's principal city, containing many marvelous illustrations and photographs.

Baxter, Nancy. *The Movers*. Indianapolis: The Guild Press, 1987. Interesting novel about several Scotch-Irish families who settled in Indiana and Kentucky.

Beeman, Richard R. *The Evolution of the Southern Backcountry: A Case Study of Lunenburg County, Virginia, 1746–1832*. Philadelphia: University of Pennsylvania Press, 1984. Interesting study of a specific area which was heavily populated by Scotch-Irish.

Bridenbaugh, Carl. *Myths and Realities: Societies of the Colonial South*. Baton Rouge: Louisiana University Press, 1952. Contains several passages about the Scotch-Irish.

Brown, P. Hume, ed. *Early Travelers in Scotland*. New York: Burt Franklin, 1891. Contains some interesting opinions of Scotland and Scotsmen.

Brunhouse, Robert L. *The Counter-Revolution in Pennsylvania, 1776–1790*. New York: Octagon Books, 1971. Contains descriptions of some of the political feuds between the Quakers and the Scotch-Irish.

The Centennial Memorial of the Presbytery of Carlisle. Augusta County, Virginia: Myers Printing and Publishing House, 1889. Contains useful information about Scotch-Irish settlers.

Chalkley, Lyman. *Chronicles of the Scotch-Irish Settlement in Virginia, Extracted From The Original Court Records of Augusta County, 1745–1800.* vol. 1 Baltimore: Genealogical Publishing, 1974. Extremely useful compilation of court records dealing with the Scotch-Irish.

Clark, Robert L. comp. *A History of the Presbytery And Its Antecedents 1732–1924.* n.p, n.d. Useful for specific information about some of the religious activities of the Scotch-Irish in Virginia.

Coleman, Terry. *Going to America.* New York: Pantheon Books, 1972. Deals with Irish and Scotch-Irish immigration from middle to late nineteenth century.

Cressey, David. *Coming Over: Migration and Communication Between England and New England in the Seventeenth Century.* Cambridge: Cambridge University Press, 1987. Deals primarily with the English, but still has some information applicable to the Scotch-Irish.

Cromie, Howard. *Ulster Settlers in America.* Belfast: Universities Press, 1976. Easy-going, highly useful account of the impact of Ulster immigrants on a developing American life.

Davidson, Chalmers G. *The Colonial Scotch-Irish of the Caroline Piedmont.* Richburg and Chester, S. C.: Chester County Genealogical Society and Chester Historical Society, 1979. Useful compilations of anecdotes by and about the Scotch-Irish.

Dickinson, R. J., *Ulster Emigration to Colonial America, 1718–1775.* London: Routledge and Kegan Paul, 1966. An informative and highly readable account of several crossings of Ulstermen to the New World.

Dinsmore, John Walker. *The Scotch-Irish in America.* Chicago: Winona Publishing, 1906. Dated, but still a valuable source for its analyses of the Scotch-Irish.

Donehoo, George P. ed. *History of the Cumberland Valley.* Harrisburg: Susquehanna History Association, 1930. Informative book about the Valley to which many Scotch-Irish migrated.

Doyle, David Noel. *Ireland, Irishmen and Revolutionary America, 1760–1820.* Dublin and Cork: The Mercier Press, 1981. Highly learned book which includes descriptions of Scotch-Irish opinions about the world they found in British North America.

Egnal, Marc. *A Mighty Empire: The Origins of the American Revolution*. Ithaca: Cornell University Press, 1988. Discusses expansionist and nonexpansionist views in reference to the American Revolution.

Finlay, Ian. *Scotland*. Oxford: Oxford University Press, 1944. A panoramic overview of Scotland and its people, with some thought provoking ideas.

Ford, Henry Jones. *The Scotch-Irish in America*. New York: Arno Press, 1967. A re-issue of a book written earlier in the century by a person who pioneered studies on the Scotch-Irish.

Garraty, John. *The American Nation: A History of the United States*. New York: Harper & Row, 1966. General U.S. history textbook that discusses immigrant groups, including the Scotch-Irish.

Gaustad, Edward Scott. *The Great Awakening in New England*. New York: Harper, 1957. Major source for information and analysis of the first Great Awakening.

Glascow, Maude. *The Scotch-Irish in Northern Ireland and in the American Colonies*. New York: G. P. Putnam & Sons, 1936. A partisan account, favoring the Protestants, of events in Ulster.

Graham, Henry Grey. *Social Life of Scotland in the 18th Century*. New York: Benjamin Bloom, 1971. Interesting book, with numerous descriptions of lifestyles and social habits.

Hanna, Charles Augustua. *The Scotch-Irish; Or The Scot in North Britain, North Ireland, and North America*. New York and London: G. P. Putnam, 1902. Dated, but still useful for its information about the Scotch-Irish, with several maps showing locations of the Scotch-Irish as they moved from place to place.

Harrison, J. Houston. *Settlers By The Long Grey Trail: A Contribution To The History and Genealogy of Colonial Families of Rockingham County, Virginia*. Baltimore: Genealogical Publishing, 1875. Useful for its statistics about some Scotch-Irish families.

Hart, Freeman Hansford. *The Valley of Virginia in the American Revolution*. Chapel Hill: University of North Carolina Press, 1942. Speaks about many Scotch-Irish who took a leading hand against the British during the Revolution.

Hastings, Sally. *A Descriptive Account of a Family Tour To the West,*

In The Year 1800, In A Letter To A Lady. Lancaster, Pennsylvania: William Dickson Printers, 1808. The author is indebted to Mary E. Karnes of Elizabethtown, Pennsylvania, for the use of this diary.

Heimert, Alan. *Religion and the American Mind From the Great Awakening to the Revolution*. Cambridge: Harvard University Press, 1966. Contains useful information about the Scotch-Irish relationship to the Great Awakening, and subsequent political events.

Hesseltine, William and Smiley, David. *The South in American History*. Englewood Cliffs, N.J.: Prentice-Hall, 1960. Discusses the Scotch-Irish, among other immigrant groups, who came into the South.

Hill, George. *An Historical Account of the Plantation of Ulster at the Commencement of the Seventeenth Century, 1606–1620*. Shannon: Irish University Press, 1877.

Hofstadter, Richard. *Anti-Intellectualism in American Life*. New York: Alfred A. Knopf, 1963. Richard Hofstadter was one of the major world historians. His books continue to be valuable to succeeding generations of historians.

Johnson, James E. *The Scots and the Scotch-Irish in America*. Minneapolis: Lerner Publications, 1966. General history of these immigrant groups.

Jones, M. G. *The Charity School Movement: A Study of Eighteenth Century Puritanism in Action*. Cambridge: Cambridge University Press, 1938. Interesting book about a movement that affected many Scotch-Irish families.

Jordon, Winthrop D. *White Over Black: American Attitudes Toward The Negro, 1550–1812*. Chapel Hill: University of North Carolina Press, 1968. Discusses where slavery was mostly concentrated in British North America.

Klett, Guy Soulliard. *Presbyterians in Colonial Pennsylvania*. Philadelphia: University of Pennsylvania Press, 1937. Useful for its discussions of why Ulstermen emigrated to America.

Lacey, Benjamin Rice. *Revivals in the Midst of the Years*. Richmond, Va.: John Knox Press, 1943. Contains some interesting stories about Scotch-Irish ministers.

Lehmann, William C. *Scottish and Scotch-Irish Contributions to Early American Life and Culture*. 2nd ed. Washington, D.C.:

Lehmann-Spohr, 1980. Discusses at length Scotch-Irish religious practices and their attitudes toward the American Revolution.

Lemon, James T. *The Best Poor Man's Country: A Geographical Study of Early Southeastern Pennsylvania*. Baltimore and London: The Johns Hopkins University Press, 1972. Valuable book, among other things, for showing the close relationship between geographical factors and historical events.

Leyburn, James G. *The Scotch-Irish: A Social History*. Chapel Hill: University of North Carolina Press, 1962. (Paperback reprint, University of North Carolina Press, 1989). A comprehensive account of the Scotch Irish as they were in Scotland, Ulster, and North America. This book is sociological in nature.

McWhiney, Grady and Jamieson, Perry. *Attack and Die: Civil War Military Tactics And The Southern Heritage*. University, Ala.: University of Alabama Press, 1982. Somewhat controversial book about Southern fighting tactics as inherited from their forebears, Scotch-Irish and otherwise.

Miller, Kerby A. *Emigrants and Exiles: Ireland and the Irish Exodus to North America*. New York: Oxford University Press, 1985. Discusses the myths that have grown up around the Scotch-Irish, but does not use all the sources available on the Scotch-Irish, namely the collections at Montreat, North Carolina, and the Presbyterian Historical Foundation in Philadelphia.

Nash, Gary B. *The Urban Crucible: Social Change, Political Consciousness, and the Origins of the American Revolution*. Cambridge: Harvard University Press, 1979. Valuable for its descriptions of Scotch-Irish who settled in urban areas.

Notestein, Wallace. *The Scots in History*. New Haven: Yale University Press, 1946. Reprint Greenwood Press, Westport, Conn.: 1970. Authoritative account of Scottish people, particularly their background and lifestyles in Scotland itself.

O'Grady, Joseph P. *How The Irish Became American*. New York: Twayne, 1973. Discusses the Southern Scotch-Irish and their involvement in the Regulator Movement.

Perceval-Maxwell, M. *The Scottish Migrations to Ulster in the Reign of James I*. London: Routledge & Kegan Paul, 1973. Scholarly and informative book dealing primarily with the first immigrations of those people who became known as the "Scotch-Irish."

Pessen, Edward. *Jacksonian America: Society, Personality, and Pol-*

itics. rev. ed. Homewood, Ill.: The Dorsey Press, 1978. A general, highly informative book dealing with a period when the Scotch-Irish and their descendants were quite active.

Posey, Walter Brownlow. *Frontier Missions: A History of Religion West of the Southern Appalachians to 1861*. Lexington: University of Kentucky Press, 1966. Discusses, among other things, the impact of Scotch-Irish Presbyterianism on the South.

———. *The Presbyterian Church in the Old Southwest, 1778–1838*. Richmond, Va.: John Knox Press, 1952. Shows the influence of the Scotch-Irish on Presbyterianism as it spread into the South.

Potter, George W. *To The Golden Door: The Story of the Irish in Ireland and America*. Westport, Conn: Greenwood Press, 1973.

Quinn, David Beers. *The Elizabethans and The Irish*. Ithaca: Cornell University Press, 1966. Useful book, especially about Irish migration patterns.

Roberts, Kenneth. *The Battle of Cowpens: The Great Morale Builder*. Garden City, N.J.: Doubleday, 1958. Description of the battle, largely won by Scotch-Irish soldiers, that Roberts claimed was a turning point in the American Revolution.

Robinson, Philip. *The Plantation of Ulster: British Settlement in an Irish Landscape, 1600–1670*. New York: St. Martin's Press, 1984. Authoritative study by a leading scholar of Ulster.

Rouse, Parke. *The Great Philadelphia Wagon Road: From Philadelphia To The South*. New York: McGraw-Hill, 1973. Highly informative book about the route followed by the Scotch-Irish and other immigrant groups to the west and south.

Rupp, Israel Daniel. *The History and Topography of Dauphin, Cumberland, Franklin, and Bedford, Adams, and Perry Counties*. Lancaster, Pa: Gilbert Hills, 1846. Contains useful information about Scotch-Irish settlers in western Pennsylvania.

Stevenson, David. *Scottish Covenanters and Irish Confederates*. Belfast: Ulster Historical Foundation, 1981.

Thompson, Ernest Trice. *Presbyterians in the South, 1607–1861*. Vol. 1. Richmond: John Knox Press, 1963. Discusses Presbyterianism during this period, including of course, the Scotch-Irish.

Trinterud, Leonard J. *The Forming Of An American Tradition: A Reexamination of Colonial Presbyterianism*. Freeport, N.Y.: Books for Libraries Press, 1949. Useful for showing the closeness of the colonial Scotch-Irish to Presbyterianism.

Turner, Herbert S. *Bethel and Her Ministers 1746–1946*. H. S. Turner, n.p., 1946. Local, privately published history, which helps to describe Presbyterians in the southern colonies and United States.

Westerkamp, Marilyn J. *Triumph of the Laity: Scots-Irish Piety and The Great Awakening, 1625–1760*. New York: Oxford University Press, 1988. Shows that Scotch-Irish immigrants brought their penchant for revivalism with them from the Old World.

Wilson, Harold McKnight. *The Lexington Presbytery Heritage*. Verona, Va: McClure Press, 1971. Local history that helps to delineate the national experiences of the Scotch-Irish.

Wittke, Carl Frederick. *We Who Built America: The Saga of the Immigrant*. New York: Prentice-Hall, 1940. Contains some interesting discussions on how the Scotch-Irish and Irish differed.

Wolf, George D. *The Fair Play Settlers of the West Branch Valley, 1769–1784: A Study of Frontier Ethnography*. Harrisburg, Pa., privately published, 1969. Another local study that helps to shed light on the national experience.

Wright, Louis B. *The Cultural Life of the American Colonies 1603–1763*. New York: Harper & Bros., 1957. Discusses how the census of 1790 has been studied by linquists to determine percentage of ethnicity.

Index